Keto

Simple and cheap low carb bread recipes for the Ketogenic Diet

A cookbook for Homemade Pizzas, crunchy Bread, Crackers and tasty Cookies

Eating Desserts and weight loss Is possible.

Maria Nutrition.

licensed professional before attempting any techniques outlined in this book.

By reading this document, the reader agrees that under no circumstances is the author responsible for any losses, direct or indirect, which are incurred as a result of the use of information contained within this document, including, but not limited to, — errors, omissions, or inaccuracies.

Table of Contents

Introduction

  Indulge In A Bit of Ketogenic History Before You Start the Journey

Chapter 1: Introduction to the Baking Process

  Baking Techniques for Perfect Bread Every Time

    You Must Get the Flour & Water Ratio Correct

    Temperature is Important

    The Finishing Touches Are Essential

    Storage for Fresh Bread

  Preparation of Yeast Bread

    Always Test The Yeast:

    Maintain The Temperature Of Rising Dough:

    Refrigerate the Yeast:

  How Much To Knead Fresh Dough:

    When The Bread Is Ready:

  Tools for Baking

  Other Useful Items

Chapter 2: Keto Bread Favorites

    Almond-Coconut Flour Bread

    Coconut Flaxseed Bread

    Cottage Bread

Dinner Rolls

Garlic Focaccia

Macadamia Bread

Pork Rind Bread

Sesame Seed Bread

Sweet Bread

Apple Cider Donut Bites

Banana Bread

Blueberry - Lemon Bread

Chocolate Croissants

Cranberry Bread - Gluten-Free

Cream Cheese Coffee Cake

Delicious Plain Cheese Croissants

Raspberry Cream Cheese Coffee Cake – Slow Cooked

Walnut Bread

Chapter 3: Keto Bagels

Almond Flour Gluten-Free Bagels

Blueberry Cream Cheese Bagels

Blueberry Yeast Bagels

Cinnamon Raisin Bagels

Cinnamon Sugar Bagels

Coconut Fathead Bagels

Coconut - Garlic Bagels

Croissant Bagels

Delicious Almond Fathead Bagels

French Toast Bagel

Mozzarella Dough Bagels

Onion Bagels

Rosemary Bagels

Sesame & Poppy Seed Bagels

Chapter 4: Keto Pizzas

Almond Flour Pizza Crust

BBQ Chicken Pizza

BBQ Meat-Lovers Pizza

Bell Pepper Pizza

Breakfast Pizza Waffles

Buffalo Chicken Crust Pizza

Margherita Keto Pizza

Pepperoni Pizza

Pizza Bites

Pocket Pizza

Sausage Crust Pizza

Thai Chicken Flatbread Pizza

Zucchini Pizza Bites

Flatbread & Pita Bread Options

Cheese Flatbread

Matzo Bread - Jewish Flatbread

Pita Pizza

Chapter 5: Keto Chips - Crackers & Breadsticks

Cheddar Parmesan Chips

Tortilla Chips

Crackers

Almond Crackers

Buttery Pesto Crackers

Chia Seed Crackers

Graham Crackers

Healthy Goat Cheese Crackers

Hemp Heart Crackers

Rosemary & Sea Salt Flax Crackers

Salty Butter Crackers

Super-Easy TJ Keto Crackers

Toasted Sesame Crackers

Breadsticks

Cheesy Garlic Breadstick Bites

Coconut & Flax Breadsticks

Italian Breadsticks

Oat Sticks

3-Way Tasty Breadsticks

Choice 1: Extra Cheesy Breadsticks

Choice 2: Italian Style Breadsticks

Choice 3: Cinnamon Sugar

Chapter 6: Keto Muffin Specialties

Sweet Options

Apple Almond Muffins

Applesauce - Cinnamon & Nutmeg Muffins

Banana & Applesauce Muffins

Blackberry Lemon Muffins

Blueberry Cream Cheese Muffins

Brownie Muffins

Chocolate Chip Covered Muffins

Chocolate Hazelnut Muffins

Chocolate Zucchini Muffins

Coconut Flour Cranberry Pumpkin Muffins

Coconut Lemon Muffins

Coffee Cake Muffins

Double-Chocolate Blender Muffins

English Muffin

French Toast Muffins

Gingerbread Blender Muffins

Lemon Poppyseed Muffins

Pancake & Berry Muffins

Pumpkin Cream Cheese Muffins

Pumpkin Maple Flaxseed Muffins

Pumpkin Spice Mug Muffin

Strawberry Glazed Muffins

Cauliflower Bacon & Cheese Muffins

Coconut Bacon Egg Muffins

Cornbread Muffins

Green Eggs & Ham Muffins

Jalapeno Muffins

Onion & Squash Muffins

Chapter 7: Keto Cookies

Almond Nut Butter Cookies

Almond Shortbread Cookies

Chocolate Macaroon Cookies With Coconut

Chocolate & Orange Cookies

Chocolate Sea Salt Cookies

Chocolate Zucchini Cookies

Cinnamon Cookies

Coconut No-Bake Cookies

Coconut & Chocolate Cookies

Dark Chocolate Chip Cookies

Italian Almond Macaroons

Italian Amaretti Cookies

Low-Carb Chocolate Chip Cookies

Orange Cream Cheese Cookies & Nuts

Peanut Butter Cookies

Peanut Butter & Jelly Cookies

Pistachio Cookies

Pumpkin Cheesecake Cookies

Snickerdoodles

Strawberry Thumbprints

Walnut Cookies

Walnut & Orange Cookies

White Chocolate Macadamia Nut Cookies

Chapter 8: A Final Word - Keto-Friendly Essentials

Grains to Avoid:

Foods Included Using The Ketogenic Plan

Excellent Keto-Friendly Flour Substitutes:

Healthy Choices For Seeds & Nuts

Dairy-Free Substitutions:

Butters:

Low-Carb Sweeteners Guide:

Other Essential Items:

Conclusion

Smoothie In A Bowl

Index For The Recipes

Description

Introduction

Congratulations on purchasing the *Keto Bread: Simple And Cheap Low-Carb Bread And Sweet Recipes For The Ketogenic Diet, A Cookbook For Homemade Pizzas, Crunchy Bread, Crackers And Tasty Cookies To Stay Healthy, Eating Delicious Desserts And Weight Loss Is Possible;* and thank you for doing so.

The following chapters will discuss how you can prepare bread and so much more. Four broad stages of bread baking are in existence when you prepare to bake and carry out the entire process. This cookbook is a short guideline of the procedures used throughout the baking cycle.

***Mixing the Recipe*:** You will be taking raw ingredients from a recipe. In the case of bread, it will consist mainly of water, flour, yeast, and salt. Next, mix them to form the dough.

***Proofing The Bread*:** Proofing is the phase of baking where the yeast eats the sugars out of the flour. The result is that it and burps out alcohol and built-up gases which causes the bread to rise and give it a natural and sweet flavor.

Baking Delicious & Healthy Bread At Home: You are 'proofing' and nurturing the dough so you can prepare a healthy meal for your family. Your primary goal is to achieve a tasty loaf of bread that both looks and tastes like it came from a professional bakery.

Baking the Bread: Baking is considered the stage where you apply the hot oven to your masterpiece. You will be creating a tasty treat.

Storing & Eating: The final phase is the easiest, just serve and enjoy the bread.

Indulge In A Bit of Ketogenic History Before You Start the Journey

During the 1920s and 1930s era, the Ketogenic diet was used medically for its role in epilepsy therapy treatments. The Ketogenic diet plan provided an alternative method other than the uncharacteristic techniques of fasting which were victorious in the treatment plan's early phases.

During the 1940s, the process was abandoned because of new therapies for seizures. However, in approximately 20 to 30% of the epileptic cases failed to control the epileptic seizures. With that failure, the Keto Diet was reintroduced as a management technique.

As time passed, the Charlie Foundation was founded by the family of Charlie Abraham in 1994 after Charlie's recovery from seizures and other health issues he suffered with daily. Charlie—as a youngster—was placed on the diet and continued to use it for five years. As of 2016, he is still functioning successfully without the seizure episodes and is furthering his education as a college student.

The Charlie Foundation appointed a panel of dietitians and neurologists to form an agreement in the form of a statement in 2006. It was written as an approval of the dieting techniques and stated which cases its use would be considered. It is noted that the plan is especially recommended for children.

Dravet Syndrome Improvements: Dravet Syndrome is a severe form of epilepsy which is marked by uncontrollable, prolonged, and frequent seizures which can begin in infancy. Available medications don't always improve symptoms, noted that in approximately one-third of Dravet Syndrome patients.

A clinical study used 13 children with Dravet Syndrome to stay on the Ketogenic diet for more than one year to remain seizure-free. Over 50% of the group decreased in the frequency of the seizures. It was reported that six of the patients stopped the diet later, but one remains seizure-free. This says a lot for the Keto methods and controlling factors.

Mental Focus Improved: Your brain is approximately 60% fat by weight. Therefore, you might become confused as you consume high-fat foods. However, by increasing your fatty food intake; you will have better chances to better your mind. It can maintain itself and work at full capacity.

You Remain Satiated: Fat and protein are more filling and will stick to your ribs longer than products which are filled with carbohydrates. Each of the bread recipes will provide you with the nutrients to remain the 'full' and 'fed' state.

These are just a few of the benefits you will achieve using the Ketogenic techniques as you enjoy your bread-baking experience.

Chapter 1: Introduction to the Baking Process

Baking Techniques for Perfect Bread Every Time

You Must Get the Flour & Water Ratio Correct

If you are following a recipe, you will have the correct ratios for preparing your bread. However, if you decide seven or eight cups isn't precise enough, the process works like this. Most sandwich bread is 2:1 flour to water. Therefore, if your dough seems to be sticky, don't be tempted to add more flour to the mixture. The result could be a loaf that will not rise.

If you don't want to take a chance of adding too much flour when preparing the work surface, you can use a light mist of cooking spray or a small amount of olive oil. Also, if your recipe doesn't call for a fat, the oil on the counter won't have an effect on the dough. You can also use some water to prevent sticky issues. Using a bench scraper, you can easily remove the dough off of the preparation surface.

Temperature is Important

It is essential to pay close attention to the temperatures when combining the ingredients into your bread. All recipe components should be around the 68-70° Fahrenheit temperature range. This method helps to keep the dough 'stretchy,' so that the bread can rise to its expected potential.

Generally speaking, proteins (such as eggs) take longer to incorporate if they are too cold. If the product is too warm, it can also lose its elasticity. The fat should be moldable and soft such as the texture of Play-Doh. You shouldn't be able to run your fingers through it. It should be malleable and not melty.

The Finishing Touches Are Essential

Some of the recipes will call for you to slash the dough. It is a process used to direct how the bread will rise when placed in the oven. Sandwich loaves should have a slash down the center. If you have a round loaf, use a tic-tac-toe board pattern, so it will evenly rise around the entire bread loaf.

Some recipes indicate you brush the dough with water, egg wash, or just egg whites. If this method is used, you can use whatever toppings you like including sesame or poppy seeds. Of course, plain is also tasty.

Storage for Fresh Bread

You will discover that many recipes don't indicate how to store bread. It is fairly simple and can be done anytime you make your bread. Store the items in the freezer. Sandwich loaves should be sliced before freezing. You can always just remove what you can eat, and save the rest for later. Consider making sandwiches for school-time lunches. You can prepare them on frozen slices and will be ready to eat by lunchtime.

Important Note: If you plan on freezing the bread, make sure it has completed its cool-down cycle. Slice and add it to freezer bags, making sure to remove all of the excess air.

Preparation of Yeast Bread

Nothing is more disappointing than the anticipation of a tasty slice of hot bread,

Only to discover that as the bread is baking; the yeast is not working. You have two common types of yeast: Active dry yeast must be dissolved in water before using. Instant yeast is mixed directly into the dough. These are a few of the guidelines to assist you through the process.

Always Test The Yeast:

If you are an avid baker and have discovered you have a package of yeast in the pantry, you can test its validity. Measure out the liquid you will be using in the recipe. Use lukewarm or room temperature water for the recipe. Empty about ½ of a cup of the mixture into a container. Drizzle the yeast along with a pinch of sugar over the top. Stir and let it rest for several minutes. The liquid will start bubbling which is a sign the yeast is still active.

Maintain The Temperature Of Rising Dough:

The best temperature for yeast is between 70º Fahrenheit to 80º Fahrenheit. You can use a warm oven (off position) or on top of the refrigerator. If your home is warm, you are already set. Think of the ways the older generations prepared such tasty bread.

Refrigerate the Yeast:

If you have purchased a hefty supply of yeast, consider placing it in the freezer compartment. It will pause the lifespan past its expiration date. Place it in an air tight container.

How Much To Knead Fresh Dough:

If your hands are tired, then the bread has probably had plenty of kneading. That conclusion and the following factors will let you know when enough is enough:

The Dough Is Smooth: You will start noticing a lumpy – shaggy mass forming as you knead. The mixture should be just slightly tacky when touched.

The Dough Holds Its Shape: Once the kneading is successful, you can hold the bread in the air, and it will maintain its form. The ball shape means the gluten is strong and tight.

Poke Test the Finished Dough: Go ahead, and poke the mixture. If the hole fills in quickly, it's ready.

Does A Windowpane Test: Pull a portion of dough (golf ball size)? Stretch it paper-thin. If it holds together, it's ready to bake. The 'true' point of kneading the dough is to strengthen the gluten (the stringy protein bands that provide

Texture to the bread). As a rule-of-thumb, it should take eight to ten minutes using a mixer or ten to twelve minutes if working the dough by hand.

When The Bread Is Ready:

- **Visually Gauge Its Doneness:** With experience, you will learn how the bread's appearance changes during the cooking cycle. The color should be a deep golden brown and firm. Don't worry about the darker spots here-and-there; it's normal for home-baked bread.

- **Check the Internal Temperature of the Bread:** Gently insert a thermometer into the center of the loaf of bread. Most bread is baked at 190º Fahrenheit.

- **Gently Tap The Bottom Of The Baking Pan:** This is a simple process. You take the pan out of the oven and turn it upside down on a flat surface. Tap the bottom, and it should sound hollow when the bread is done. Towards the end of the baking cycle, you can try this method every five minutes.

Tools for Baking

The most essential tools for baking bread are the oven and your hands. If you learned baking techniques used by your Grandma, you add the bread to the countertop and do the kneading right there. However, for most individuals now, you will use a heavy-duty large mixing container that hasn't got a slippery bottom. You can use a damp towel to complete the task.

An unglazed terra cotta tile in the bottom of a clean oven or a baking stone might be a good investment if you are planning on doing a lot of baking at home. You can also purchase an upgraded stand mixer with a dough hook. It's also a good idea to purchase several different sized loaf pans.

You should also invest in several mixing bowls to use. A bench knife, better known as a dough scraper, can be used to clean surfaces, divide the dough, and to pre-shape the loaves of bread. Some even use it to dice veggies and apples.

These are a few additional items that will assist you with the baking process:

- Electric mixer/food processor
- Measuring cups (liquid and dry)
- Medium to large-sized saucepans
- Rubber spatula
- Rolling pin
- Wire cooling rack
- Bread or cutting board
- Plastic wrap – damp tea towel
- Parchment baking paper

Other Useful Items

Kitchen Scales: It is almost a necessity to own a set of food scales to take out the guesswork. Keep the following in mind before you make the purchase:

- **Seek a Conversion Button:** You need to know how to convert measurements into grams since not all recipes have them listed. The grams keep the system in complete harmony.

- **The Tare Function:** When you set a bowl on the scale, the feature will allow you to reset the scale back to zero (0).

- **Removable Plate:** Keep the germs off of the scale by removing the plate. Be sure it will come off to eliminate the bacterial buildup.

Now that you have the basics, let's start baking a delicious treat!

Chapter 2: Keto Bread Favorites

Almond-Coconut Flour Bread

Servings Provided: 8

Cooking & Prep Time: 50-55 min.

Macro Counts For Each Serving:

- **Protein**: 5 g
- **Fat Content**: 13 g
- **Calories**: 161
- **Total Net Carbs**: 3 g

Ingredient List:

- Eggs (6)
- Coconut oil (.33 cup)
- Unsweetened almond milk (.33 cup)
- Salt (.25 tsp.)
- Xanthan gum (1 tsp.)
- Coconut flour (.5 cup)
- Baking powder (1 tbsp.)

Prep Technique:

1. Warm up the oven to reach 350° Fahrenheit.
2. Whisk the coconut oil with the milk and eggs.
3. Sift and mix in the baking powder, coconut flour, and salt.
4. Stir until it has thickened.
5. In a greased bread pan, spread the mixture evenly.
6. Bake for 35 to 40 minutes.
7. Allow the bread to cool slightly before serving.

Coconut Flaxseed Bread

Servings Provided: 8

Cooking & Prep Time: 50 min.

Macro Counts For Each Serving:

- **Protein**: 9.2 g
- **Fat Content**: 8.5 g
- **Calories**: 154
- **Total Net Carbs**: 3.8g

Ingredient List:

- Bak. soda (.5 tsp.)
- Flaxseed meal (.5 cup)
- Sifted coconut flour (1 cup)
- Salt (1 tsp.)
- Bak. powder (1 tsp.)
- Unchilled large eggs (6)
- Water (.5 cup)
- Apple cider vinegar (1 tbsp.)

Prep Technique:

1. Warm the oven in advance to 350° Fahrenheit.
2. Lightly grease a baking pan of choice.
3. Sift or whisk the flour into a mixing container. Add and mix the remainder of dry fixings.
4. Pour in the vinegar and water to form a thick batter. Press the mixture into a prepared pan.
5. Bake until browned or for about 40 minutes.
6. Cool in the pan until slightly warm and remove. Slice and serve.

Cottage Bread

Servings Provided: 6

Cooking & Prep Time: 65 min.

Macro Counts For Each Serving:

- **Protein**: 8.4 g
- **Fat Content**: 6.3 g
- **Calories**: 109
- **Total Net Carbs**: 6 g

Ingredient List:

- Ground sesame seeds (1 tsp.)
- Ground flaxseed (1 tsp.)
- Egg (1)
- Cottage cheese (7-8 oz.)
- Turmeric powder (.125 or to taste)
- Salt (1 pinch)
- Baking powder (.5 tsp.)
- Sunflower seeds (1.5-2 oz.)
- Wheat bran (2 tbsp.)
- Oat bran (3 tbsp.)

Prep Technique:

1. Warm up the oven to reach 425° Fahrenheit.

2. Add a sheet of parchment paper to the baking dish.

3. Combine the sesame seeds, flaxseed, egg, and cottage cheese. Shake in the salt and turmeric. Fold in the seeds, oat bran, and wheat bran.

4. Stir well and let the mixture rest for 10 minutes.

5. Shape the mixture into a ball.

6. Bake for 45 minutes in the hot oven. Remove and cool.

7. *Note:* Wet your hands with a small amount of water so the dough mixture doesn't stick to you while you prepare the bread.

Dinner Rolls

Servings Provided: 6 rolls

Cooking & Prep Time: 30 min.

Macro Counts For Each Serving:

- **Protein**: 10.7 g
- **Fat Content**: 18 g
- **Calories**: 219
- **Total Net Carbs**: 2.3 g

Ingredient List:

- Mozzarella (1 cup - shredded)

- Cream cheese (1 oz.)
- Almond flour (1 cup)
- Ground flaxseed (.25 cup)
- Egg (1)
- Baking soda (.5 tsp.)

Prep Technique:

1. Warm the oven to reach 400° Fahrenheit.
2. Prepare a baking pan with a sheet of parchment paper.
3. Melt the mozzarella and cream cheese together (microwave for 1 min.).
4. Stir well and add a whisked egg. Combine well.
5. In another container, whisk the baking soda, almond flour, and flaxseed. Mix in the cheese mixture to form a sticky soft-ball.
6. Dampen your hands with water and roll the dough into six balls.
7. Roll the tops in sesame seeds and place on the baking sheet.
8. Bake until nicely browned (10-12 min.).
9. Cool 15 minutes and serve.

Garlic Focaccia No

Servings Provided: 8

Cooking & Prep Time: 40 min.

Macro Counts For Each Serving:

- **Protein**: 10 g
- **Fat Content**: 19 g
- **Calories**: 245
- **Total Net Carbs**: 3.4 g

Ingredient List:

- Almond flour (1 cup)
- Bak. powder (1 tsp.)
- Ground flaxseed (1 cup)
- Eggs (6)
- Olive oil (.25 cup)
- Minced cloves of garlic (2)
- Basil (1 tsp.)
- Salt (2 pinches)
- Dried oregano (1 tsp.)
- 8x8 glass baking dish

Prep Technique:

1. Heat the oven to reach 350º Fahrenheit.

2. Sift or whisk the flour in with the spices, baking powder, and flaxseed into a mixing container.
3. One by one, add the eggs and garlic, whisking as you go.
4. Pour in the oil and combine the batter.
5. Line the baking dish with a sheet of baking paper and add the batter.
6. Bake for 25 minutes and serve or cool to store.

Macadamia Bread

Servings Provided: 16

Cooking & Prep Time: 50 min.

Macro Counts For Each Serving:
- **Protein**: 5 g
- **Fat Content**: 22 g
- **Calories**: 227
- **Total Net Carbs**: 5 g

Ingredient List:
- Macadamia nuts (2 cups)
- Eggs (4)
- Almond flour (.25 cup)
- Ground flaxseed (2 tbsp.)
- Softened ghee (.25 cup)

- Softened coconut butter (.5 cup)
- Sea salt (1 tsp.)
- Baking powder (.5 tsp.)
- Apple cider vinegar (2 tbsp.)
- *Also Needed*: 8x4 loaf pan

Prep Technique:

1. Warm the oven before baking time to 350º Fahrenheit.
2. Lightly grease the pan with ghee.
3. Process the nuts using the food processor until they are fine flour.
4. Add the eggs - 1 at a time – with the motor running until the mixture is creamy.
5. Fold in the flaxseed, almond flour, coconut butter, ghee, vinegar, sea salt, and baking powder. Continue processing until well combined.
6. Scoop into the oiled bread pan.
7. Bake for 35 to 40 minutes. Cool the bread before slicing to serve or store.

Pork Rind Bread

Servings Provided: 12

Cooking & Prep Time: 50-55 min.

Macro Counts For Each Serving:

- **Protein**: 9 g
- **Fat Content**: 13 g
- **Calories**: 166
- **Total Net Carbs**: 1.9 g

Ingredient List:

- Cream cheese (8 oz.)
- Mozzarella cheese grated (2 cups)
- Eggs (3 large)
- Parmesan cheese grated (.25 cup)
- Crushed pork rinds (1 cup)
- Baking powder (1 tbsp.)
- Herbs and spices (to taste)

Prep Technique:

1. Set the oven temperature to reach 375º Fahrenheit.
2. Prepare a baking tin with parchment baking paper.
3. Place both types of cheese into a microwave-safe dish.
4. Microwave the cheese mixture using the high-power setting for one minute.
5. Stir and microwave for another minute.

6. Fold in the egg with the parmesan, baking powder, and pork rinds. Stir until all ingredients have been incorporated.
7. Spread onto the pan.
8. Bake for 15-20 minutes. Add the pan to a cooling rack for about 15 minutes. Transfer from the pan at that time and finish cooling.

Sesame Seed Bread

Servings Provided: 6

Cooking & Prep Time: 1 hr. 30 min.

Macro Counts For Each Serving:

- **Protein**: 7 g
- **Fat Content**: 13 g
- **Calories**: 100
- **Total Net Carbs**: 1 g

Ingredient List:

- Sesame seeds (2 tbsp.)
- Psyllium husk powder (5 tbsp.)
- Sea salt (.25 tsp.)
- Apple cider vinegar (2 tsp.)
- Almond flour (1.25 cups)
- Bak. powder (2 tsp.)

- Boiling water (1 cup)
- Egg whites (3)

Prep Technique:

1. Heat the oven ahead of baking time to reach 350º Fahrenheit.
2. Spritz a baking tin with some cooking oil spray. Put the water in a saucepan to boil.
3. Mix the baking powder, almond flour, sea salt, sesame seeds, and psyllium powder.
4. Stir in the hot water, vinegar, and egg whites. Use a hand mixer (less than 1 min.) to combine. Place the bread on the prepared pan.
5. Bake for 1 hour on the lowest rack. Serve and enjoy any time.

Sweet Bread

Apple Cider Donut Bites

Servings Provided: 12 - 2 bites each
Cooking & Prep Time: 30 min.
Macro Counts For Each Serving:

- **Protein**: 6.5 g
- **Fat Content**: 17.7 g
- **Calories**: 164

- **Total Net Carbs**: 2.6 g

Ingredient List - The Bites:
- Almond flour (2 cups)
- Cinnamon (.5 tsp.)
- Swerve sweetener (.5 cup)
- Plain whey protein powder (.25 cup)
- Bak. powder (2 tsp.)
- Salt (.5 tsp.)
- Large eggs (2)
- Water (.33 cup)
- Butter - melted (.25 cup)
- Apple cider vinegar (1.5 tbsp.)
- Apple extract (1.5 tsp.)

Ingredient List - The Coating:
- Swerve sweetener (.25 cup)
- Cinnamon (1-2 tsp.)
- Melted butter (.25 cup)
- *Also Needed*: 24- count mini muffin pan

Prep Technique:

1. Set the oven to 325° Fahrenheit. Lightly grease the pan.
2. Whisk the almond flour, protein powder, sweetener, baking powder, cinnamon, and salt.
3. Whisk the eggs and water with the butter, apple cider vinegar, and apple extract. Combine the fixings.
4. Divide the mixture among the wells of the pan.
5. Bake until the muffins are firm to the touch (15-20 min.). Then, cool for about ten minutes on a wire rack.
6. In a small container, whisk together the sweetener and cinnamon.
7. Dip each donut bite into the melted butter, coating completely.
8. Roll each donut bite into the cinnamon/sweetener mixture.

Banana Bread

Servings Provided: 16

Cooking & Prep Time: 1 hr. 25 min.

Macro Counts For Each Serving:

- **Protein**: 4 g
- **Fat Content**: 15 g
- **Calories**: 165
- **Total Net Carbs**: 8 g

Ingredient List:

- Bak. powder (1 tsp.)
- Stevia (.25 tsp.)
- Salt (.5 tsp.)
- Xanthan gum (.5 tsp.)
- Almond flour (.75 cup)
- Coconut flour (.33 cup)
- Vanilla extract (1 tsp.)
- Medium eggs (6)
- Erythritol (.5 cup)
- Coconut oil (3 tbsp.)
- Medium banana (1)
- Melted butter (.5 cup)

Prep Technique:

1. Warm the oven to reach 325º Fahrenheit.
2. Grease a loaf pan.
3. Sift or whisk the almond and coconut flour, xanthan gum, stevia, salt, erythritol, and baking powder.
4. Slice the banana, and add to a food processor with the butter, oil, eggs, and vanilla extract. Pulse for one minute and combine with the rest of the fixings. Pulse for one additional minute until well blended.
5. Empty into the pan.
6. Bake for 1 hr. 15 min. Serve.

Blueberry - Lemon Bread

Servings Provided: 10

Cooking & Prep Time: 60 min.

Macro Counts For Each Serving:
- **Protein**: 9 g
- **Fat Content**: 17 g
- **Calories**: 207
- **Total Net Carbs**: 5 g

Ingredient List:

- Blueberries (1 cup)
- Lemon zested (1)
- Vanilla extract (.5 tsp.)
- Lemon extract (1 tbsp.)
- Dairy-free mayonnaise (3 tbsp.)
- Medium egg whites (2)
- Whole large eggs (6)
- Salt (.25 tsp.)
- Baking soda (.5 tsp.)
- Almond flour (2 cups)
- Cream of tartar (1 tsp.)
- Coconut flour (.25 cups)
- Stevia (.75 cups)

Prep Technique:

1. Warm the oven to reach 350º Fahrenheit.
2. Prepare the bread pan with a layer of parchment paper.
3. Whisk the almond flour, salt, baking soda, stevia, and coconut flour.
4. Fold in the egg whites, whole eggs, mayonnaise, lemon and vanilla extract, and lemon zest.
5. Combine well with an electric mixer.
6. Stir in half of the berries (.5 cup) and add to the prepared pan. Bake for 20 minutes.

7. Top it off with the remainder of the berries when it is through the first baking. Continue baking for an additional 50 minutes.

8. Transfer to the counter to cool for about two hours. Serve any time.

Chocolate Croissants

Servings Provided: 6

Cooking & Prep Time: 30 min.

Macro Counts for Each Serving:

- **Protein**: 10 g
- **Fat Content**: 18 g
- **Calories**: 218
- **Total Net Carbs**: 3 g

Ingredient List:

- Shredded mozzarella (1.5 cups)
- Almond flour (.75 cup)
- Cream cheese (2 tbsp.)
- Egg (1)
- Low-carb sweetener - ex. Lakanto (2 tbsp.)
- Lily's Original Dark Chocolate (1.5 oz.)

Prep Technique:

1. Warm the oven to reach 350° Fahrenheit. Place a silicone baking mat on a baking pan.
2. Place the mozzarella and cream cheese in the microwaveable bowl.
3. Set the timer for one minute. Stir and cook for another 30 seconds.
4. Whisk the egg, sweetener, and almond flour. Combine all of the fixings.
5. Let the dough cool slightly, and then knead until smooth. Add a *little* extra almond flour if the dough is too sticky, and then knead again.
6. Portion the dough into six balls. Slightly flatten each ball in your hand and place two small pieces of chocolate across the center.
7. Fold the dough over the top and press to seal it closed.
8. Arrange them on the baking sheet.
9. Bake for 14 to 20 minutes. Leave to cool slightly in the pan for about five minutes before serving.

Cranberry Bread - Gluten-Free

Servings Provided: 12

Cooking & Prep Time: 1 hr. 45-50 min.

Macro Counts for Each Serving:

- **Protein**: 6.4 g
- **Fat Content**: 15 g
- **Calories**: 179
- **Total Net Carbs**: 4.7g

Ingredient List:

- Almond flour (2 cups)
- Powdered erythritol or Swerve (.5 cup)
- Steviva stevia powder (.5 tsp.)
- Bak. Powder (1.5 tsp.)
- Bak. Soda (.5 tsp.)
- Salt (1 tsp.)
- Unsalted butter melted or coconut oil (4 tbsp.)
- Eggs at room temperature (4 large)
- Coconut milk (.5 cup)
- Cranberries (12 oz. bag)
- *Optional*: Blackstrap molasses (1 tsp.)
- *Also Needed*: 9x5 loaf pan

Prep Technique:

1. Set the oven temperature to 350º Fahrenheit. Rinse the cranberries.
2. Sift the flour, baking soda, erythritol or stevia, salt, and baking powder.

3. In another container, combine the eggs, butter, molasses, and coconut milk.

4. Combine it all until well combined.

5. It's important to lightly grease the baking pan before you start baking.

6. Fold in the berries and add to the pan. Bake about 1.25 hours.

7. Place the pan on a wire rack to cool (15 min.) before removing from the pan.

8. *Note:* Watch closely when you approach the 1-hour marker since oven temperatures vary.

Cream Cheese Coffee Cake

Servings Provided: 8

Cooking & Prep Time: 50-60 min.

Macro Counts for Each Serving:

- **Protein**: 13 g
- **Fat Content**: 28 g
- **Calories**: 321
- **Total Net Carbs**: 4.2 g

Ingredient List:

- Eggs (6 separated)
- Cream cheese (6 oz.)

- Erythritol (.25 cup)
- Liquid stevia (.25 tsp.)
- Unflavored protein powder (.25 cup)
- Cream of tartar (.25 tsp.)
- Vanilla extract (2 tsp.)

Ingredient List - The Filling:
- Cinnamon (1 tbsp.)
- Almond flour (1.5 cups)
- Butter (.5 stick)
- Maple syrup substitute (.25 cup)
- Erythritol (.25 cup)
- *Also Needed*: Dark metal cake pan

Prep Technique:
1. Warm the oven in advance to 325° Fahrenheit.
2. Separate the yolks from the whites of the eggs.
3. Whisk the egg yolks with the erythritol and add with the rest of the fixings. (Omit the egg whites and cream of tartar for the next step.)
4. Whisk the tartar and whites of the eggs to create stiff peaks. Gently work into the yolks.
5. Mix all of the filling fixings to form the dough.

6. Scoop the batter base into the pan. Top it off with half of the cinnamon filling, pushing it down if needed.
7. Bake for 20 minutes. Transfer to the countertop and top the cake off with the rest of the filling dough.
8. Bake for another 20 minutes to half an hour. Cool for 10 to 20 minutes before serving.

Delicious Plain Cheese Croissants

Servings Provided: 8

Cooking & Prep Time: 23 min.

Macro Counts for Each Serving:

- **Protein**: 16 g
- **Fat Content**: 17.2 g
- **Calories**: 248
- **Total Net Carbs**: 3.4g

Ingredient List:

- Shredded mozzarella cheese (3 cups)
- Cream cheese (2 oz.)
- Eggs (3 whites)
- Coconut flour (.5 cup)
- Melted butter (2 tbsp.)

- Psyllium husk (1 tbsp.)
- Sparkling water (2 tbsp.)
- Salt (as desired)
- *Also Needed*: Baking tin lined with parchment baking paper

Prep Technique:

1. Warm up the oven to 385° Fahrenheit.
2. Prepare a baking sheet with a layer of the paper.
3. Whisk just the whites of the eggs until soft peaks form.
4. Add the mozzarella and cream cheese into a mixing bowl. Stir and microwave until melted.
5. Whisk and fold in the egg whites, coconut flour, psyllium husk, and a pinch of salt.
6. Knead with your hands until a dough-like consistency is reached. Add sparkling water, and continue kneading.
7. Place the prepared dough between two layers of baking paper. Spread it and begin flattening with a rolling pin to about 1/3-inch thickness.
8. Brush half of the melted butter onto the dough.
9. With a pizza cutter, start dividing the dough into four equal squares and further cut each square

into two triangles that have a bottom approximately 4 inches wide.

10. Roll the triangles upward, starting at the widest part, and gradually curve into a crescent shape.

11. Place the croissants onto baking sheet at least 2 inches apart.

12. Brush the remaining butter on top.

13. Set the timer for 12 minutes. Bake until golden brown.

Notes: Before you begin, bring the water to room temperature. If the

Dough becomes hard; microwave it for 10 to 15 seconds. This is a great option, but keep in mind it is a little on the 'doughy' side.

Raspberry Cream Cheese Coffee Cake – Slow Cooked

Servings Provided: 12

Cooking & Prep Time: 4 hr. 30 min.

Macro Counts for Each Serving:

- **Protein**: 7.5 g
- **Fat Content**: 19.2 g
- **Calories**: 239

- **Total Net Carbs**: 3.9 g

Ingredient List:
- Swerve sweetener (.5 cup)
- Almond flour (1.25 cups)
- Salt (.25 tsp.)
- Vanilla protein powder (.25 cup)
- Coconut flour (25 cups)
- Baking powder (1.5 tsp.)
- Water (.66 cup)
- Melted organic butter (6 tbsp.)
- Vanilla extract (.5 tsp.)
- Large eggs (3)

Ingredient List - The Filling:
- Powdered Swerve sweetener (.33 cup)
- Organic cream cheese (8 oz.)
- Large egg (1)
- Fresh raspberries (1.5 cups)
- Organic whipping cream (2 tbsp.)
- *Suggested Size Of Cooker*: 6-quart

Prep Technique:
1. Grease the insert of the cooker thoroughly and prepare the batter.

2. Combine the dry fixings. Stir in the melted butter, eggs, and water.

3. Prepare the filling. Whip the sweetener and cream cheese until smooth. Whisk the whipping cream, vanilla extract, and egg until well mixed.

4. Assemble the cake using 2/3 of the batter poured into the cooker.

5. Smooth the batter and add the cream cheese mixture. Sprinkle with the berries. Use a spoon to 'dot' the top of the cake mixture.

6. Prepare for three to four hours on the low setting or until the edges are browned. The filling may still have a little jiggle if shaken.

7. Turn off the slow cooker and remove the insert.

8. Let it cool before serving.

Walnut Bread

Servings Provided: 10

Cooking & Prep Time: 1 hr. 14 min.

Macro Counts for Each Serving:

- **Protein**: 8 g
- **Fat Content**: 22 g
- **Calories**: 269
- **Total Net Carbs**: 11 g

Ingredient List:

- Olive oil (.25 cup)
- Coconut oil (for the pan)
- Medium bananas (3)
- Eggs (3 large)
- Walnuts (.5 of 1 cup)
- Almond flour (2 cups)
- Bak. Soda (1 tsp.)

Prep Technique:

1. Warm the oven in advance to 350º Fahrenheit.
2. Lightly grease the pan with coconut oil.
3. Slice the bananas into circles, and add to a mixing bowl with the rest of the fixings. Use the blender (high setting) to prepare the batter.
4. Empty the batter into a loaf pan. Bake for 50 to 60 minutes.
5. Cool slightly. Serve warm.

Chapter 3: Keto Bagels

Almond Flour Gluten-Free Bagels

Servings Provided: 8

Cooking & Prep Time: 35 min.

Macro Counts for Each Serving:

- **Protein**: 19 g
- **Fat Content**: 21 g
- **Calories**: 289
- **Total Net Carbs**: 2 g

Ingredient List:

- Almond flour (1.5 cups)

- Baking powder - gluten-free (2 tsp.)
- Eggs (2)
- Cream cheese (2 oz.)
- Shredded mozzarella cheese (3 cups)
- Everything But the Bagel Seasoning (see below)

Ingredient List - Homemade Everything But The Bagel Seasoning:

- Black sesame seeds (1.5 tsp.)
- Poppy seeds (.5 tsp.)
- White sesame seeds (2 tsp.)
- Dried minced onion (1 tsp.)
- Sea salt or kosher salt (1 tsp.)
- Dried minced garlic (1 tsp.)

Prep Technique:

1. Warm the oven to reach 400° Fahrenheit.
2. Prepare a baking sheet with parchment paper or a silicone baking mat.
3. Whisk the baking powder and almond flour.
4. In a microwavable container, toss the cream cheese and shredded mozzarella, and microwave for 60 seconds.

5. Remove the bowl and stir in the almond flour. (Microwave at 30-second intervals if it's too thick to stir.)
6. Stir and add the egg to form the dough. Knead the dough with your hands to form one large ball.
7. Scoop out 8 balls of dough, roll, and add to the baking mat.
8. Create a circle in the middle of each ball. Check the bagels while they are in the oven. If you see the circles closing up, use a knife to open them back up.
9. Remove and slightly dampen the tops with a small amount of water and sprinkle with the seasoning.
10. Bake until golden brown or for about 15 to 20 minutes.

Blueberry Cream Cheese Bagels

Servings Provided: 12

Cooking & Prep Time: 25-32 min.

Macro Counts for Each Serving:

- **Protein**: 3.8 g
- **Fat Content**: 5.1 g
- **Calories**: 68
- **Total Net Carbs**: 2.8 g

Ingredient List:
- Shredded mozzarella cheese (2.5 cups)
- Almond flour (.75 cup)
- Nut flour (.75 cup)
- Cream cheese (2 oz.)
- Eggs (2)
- Egg for egg wash (1)
- Fresh blueberries (.5 cup)
- Baking powder (1 tbsp.)
- Erythritol - separated (2 tsp.)

Prep Technique:
1. Warm the oven in advance to reach 400° Fahrenheit.
2. Add the mozzarella cheese and cream cheese together. Melt in a double boiler or microwave.
3. In another container, mix the almond flour, baking powder, \\\\ and 1 teaspoon of erythritol and set aside.
4. When the cheese mixture is melted, add 2 eggs and mix well.
5. Pour the flour mixture into the egg and cheese mixture.
6. Knead until all ingredients are fully blended.
7. Carefully fold in the blueberries.

8. Divide the dough into 8 balls. Roll into balls to form a log.

9. Pinch ends together to form a circle and place on a baking sheet.

10. Brush the bagels with egg wash.

11. Sprinkle the tops with the remainder of the erythritol.

12. Bake for 10 to 14 minutes. Transfer onto a cooling rack to cool slightly before serving.

Blueberry Yeast Bagels

Servings Provided: 8

Cooking & Prep Time: 40 min.

Macro Counts for Each Serving:

- **Protein**: 6 g
- **Fat Content**: 15 g
- **Calories**: 197
- **Total Net Carbs**: 3.5g

Ingredient List:

- Blueberries (.5-1 cup) **
- Active dry yeast (1 tbsp.)
- Maple syrup (2 tsp.)
- Apple cider vinegar (1 tbsp.)

- Lukewarm water (.5 cup)
- Almond flour (2 cups)
- Golden flaxseed meal/finely ground psyllium husk (.33 cup)
- Whey protein isolate/more almond flour (.25 cup)
- Golden erythritol - not xylitol (.33 cup)
- Xanthan gum (2.5 tsp.) or Ground flax seeds (1.5 tbsp.)**
- Baking powder (2 tsp.)
- Cinnamon (.5 tsp.)
- Kosher salt (.5-.75 tsp.)
- Unchilled egg (1)
- Unchilled egg whites (2)
- Olive oil (1.5 tbsp.)

Ingredient List - The Toppings:
- Egg white (1)
- Golden erythritol (2 tbsp.)
- Cinnamon (.5-1 tsp.)

Prep Technique:
1. Warm the oven to 350° Fahrenheit. Prepare a baking tin with parchment paper or a silicone mat.

2. Add the yeast and maple syrup into a mixing container.

3. Boil water to 105-110° Fahrenheit - slightly warm to touch, and add to the yeast mixture. Use a kitchen towel to cover the bowl for seven minutes. (If the mixture is not bubbly, it means the yeast isn't working. You need to start over.)

4. Combine the psyllium husk/flaxseed meal, almond flour, erythritol, xanthan gum, whey protein isolate, baking powder, salt, and cinnamon into another mixing container. Whisk well and set aside.

5. After the yeast is proofed, stir in the eggs, vinegar, and oil. Mix until light and frothy using an electric mixer or a whisk (2-3 min.).

6. Prepare the flour mixture in two batches until fully combined. Fold in the blueberries.

7. Divide the dough into eight balls. Smooth them out as much as possible. Stretch out the dough until bagel-shaped.

8. Wrap the dough with an oiled cling film (ex. Saran Wrap) and place in a draft-free warm space for 20 to 60 minutes (20 min. = denser bagel and 40-60 min. = fluffier bagel).

9. Lightly beat the egg white with a teaspoon of water for the egg wash.

10. Brush the bagels with the egg white wash, sprinkle with toppings of choice, and bake for about 20-25 minutes. Check for doneness at the halfway marker. Cover with foil if needed.

11. Remove and cool completely for best texture (15 min.).

12. **Use either frozen or fresh blueberries. Just thaw and let them become room temperature.

Cinnamon Raisin Bagels

Servings Provided: 6
Cooking & Prep Time: 35-40 min.
Macro Counts for Each Serving:

- **Protein**: 3 g
- **Fat Content**: 10 g
- **Calories**: 139
- **Total Net Carbs**: 6 g

Ingredient List:

- Sifted coconut flour (.33 cup)
- Golden flax meal (1.5 tbsp.)

- Bak. Soda (.5 tsp.)
- *Optional:* Sea salt (a dash)
- Bak. Powder (1 tsp.)
- Cinnamon (2 tsp.)
- Whisked eggs (3)
- Apple cider vinegar (1 tsp.)
- Unsweetened coconut/almond milk (.33 cup)
- Melted butter - coconut oil or ghee (2.5 tbsp.)
- Liquid stevia (1 tsp.)
- Golden raisins (.33 cup)
- *Optional*: Vanilla extract (1 tsp.)
- *Also Needed:* Donut/bagel pan

Prep Technique:

1. Warm the oven ahead of baking time to 350º Fahrenheit.
2. Grease the pan.
3. Mix the dry fixings thoroughly (the golden flax meal, sifted coconut flour, baking soda, cinnamon, sea salt, and baking powder).
4. In another container, combine the almond/coconut milk, apple cider vinegar, eggs, melted butter/coconut oil, vanilla extract, and stevia.

5. Combine all of the fixings and add to the prepared pan – spreading evenly with a spatula.

6. Bake for 17 to 20 minutes. Cool for three to four minutes.

7. Loosen the bagels with a knife. Turn the bread on the side and slice into half.

8. Serve with toppings of your choice such as butter or cream cheese.

9. Refrigerate or freeze unused portions.

Cinnamon Sugar Bagels

Servings Provided: 6 bagels

Cooking & Prep Time: 40 min.

Macro Counts for Each Serving:

- **Protein**: 25.4 g
- **Fat Content**: 19.9 g
- **Calories**: 317
- **Total Net Carbs**: 5.6 g

Ingredient List:

- Almond flour (1.75 cups)
- Cream of tartar (2 tsp.)
- Coconut flour (.25 cup)
- Baking soda (1 tsp.)

- Lakanto golden monk fruit sweetener - divided (3 tbsp.)
- Cinnamon - divided (1 tbsp.)
- Shredded mozzarella (2.5 cups)
- Cream cheese (2 oz.)
- Large eggs (3)

Prep Technique:

1. Set the oven temperature to 400° Fahrenheit and prepare a baking sheet using a layer of parchment baking paper.
2. Whisk one tablespoon of the monk fruit sweetener, coconut flour, baking soda, almond flour, cream of tartar, and one teaspoon of cinnamon.
3. Add the mozzarella and cream cheese into a microwave-safe bowl. Cook for 90 seconds. Remove the dish carefully and stir the fixings.
4. Return to cook for another 60 seconds. Stir well to combine.
5. In another container, whisk two eggs, and add to the large container of flour. Pour the cheese mixture in with the eggs and flour. Knead the dough and divide into six portions, connecting the

two ends to create the bagels. Place onto the baking sheet.

6. In another container, whisk the last egg. Using a pastry brush, cover each of the bagels. Mix the cinnamon and remainder of the sweetener to sprinkle over the tops.

7. Bake for 12 to 14 minutes.

8. When ready, cool for a minimum of 15 minutes.

Coconut Fathead Bagels

Servings Provided: 2

Cooking & Prep Time: 25-30 min.

Macro Counts for Each Serving:

- **Protein**: 14 g
- **Fat Content**: 16 g
- **Calories**: 234
- **Total Net Carbs**: 4 g

Ingredient List:

- Coconut flour (.5 cup)
- Aluminum-free baking powder (2 tbsp.)
- Cream cheese (2 oz.)
- Shredded mozzarella cheese (2.5 cups)
- Melted butter (2 tbsp.)

Prep Technique:

1. Set the oven temperature to 400° Fahrenheit.
2. Prepare a baking pan with a sheet of parchment baking paper.
3. Whisk or sift the coconut flour and the baking powder into a mixing container.
4. Melt the mozzarella and cream cheese for one minute using high power in the microwave. Stir and cook for another minute.
5. Mix in the beaten eggs, butter, and coconut flour mixture to form the dough.
6. Divide the dough into six segments. Roll and form the bagel.
7. Place the bagels on the baking tin. Bake until lightly browned (approx. 12 to 16 min.). Serve.

Coconut - Garlic Bagels

Servings Provided: 6

Cooking & Prep Time: 40 min.

Macro Counts for Each Serving:

- **Protein**: 8 g
- **Fat Content**: 16 g
- **Calories**: 191

- **Total Net Carbs**: 3 g

Ingredient List:

- Melted butter (.33 cup)
- Sifted coconut flour (.5 cup)
- Bak. Powder (.5 tsp.)
- Guar gum or xanthan gum - optional (2 tsp.)
- Eggs (6)
- Salt (.5 tsp.)
- Garlic powder (1.5 tsp.)

Prep Technique:

1. Heat the oven at 400° Fahrenheit.
2. Lightly grease the pan.
3. Blend together the eggs, butter, salt, and garlic powder.
4. Combine the coconut flour, baking powder, and guar/xanthan gum.
5. Whisk the coconut flour mixture into the batter until there are no lumps.
6. Scoop into the pan. Bake for 15 minutes.
7. Cool on a rack for 10-15 minutes.
8. Transfer the bagels from the pan to cool or serve. Store in the fridge.

Croissant Bagels

Servings Provided: 7

Cooking & Prep Time: 25 min.

Macro Counts for Each Serving:

- **Protein**: 3.4 g
- **Fat Content**: 6.8 g
- **Calories**: 83
- **Total Net Carbs**: 1.1 g

Ingredient List:

- Eggs (3 separated)
- Cream of tartar (.25 tsp.)
- Softened cream cheese (2 tbsp.)
- Melted butter (2 tbsp.)
- Coconut flour (2 tbsp.)
- Sweetener of choice:1.5 tsp. erythritol/15 drops liquid stevia
- Baking soda (.5 tsp. + .25 tsp. . .cream of tartar mixed together in separate pinch bowl)
- Sea salt (.125 tsp.)
- *Also Needed*: 1 donut pan or bagel pan

Prep Technique:

1. Set the oven to 300° Fahrenheit. Spritz a bagel or donut pan with some cooking oil spray.
2. Separate the egg whites from the yolks, and place into individual containers.
3. Add cream of tartar to the egg whites and whip until stiff peaks form. Set aside.
4. Beat the egg yolks in another mixing container and add the melted butter, cream cheese, sweetener of choice, baking soda, sea salt, coconut flour, and cream of tartar mixture. Beat the egg yolk mixture until fully combined.
5. Gently fold the egg yolk mixture into the egg white mixture until combined (whipped meringue texture).
6. Spoon the batter into a bagel pan.
7. Bake until the tops and edges are slightly browning (20 to 25 min.).
8. Remove and cool. If needed, loosen with a butter knife.

Delicious Almond Fathead Bagels

Servings Provided: 6

Cooking & Prep Time: 26-30 min.

Macro Counts for Each Serving:

- **Protein**: 20 g
- **Fat Content**: 31 g
- **Calories**: 377
- **Total Net Carbs**: 5 g

Ingredient List:
- Almond flour (1.5 cups)
- Mozzarella cheese (2.5 cups)
- Cream cheese (3 oz.)
- Eggs (2)
- Egg white - beaten with a little water (1)
- Baking powder (1 tbsp.)
- Salt (.25 tsp.)
- Flavorless oil (1 tsp.)
- *Optional:* Everything Bagel Seasoning
- *Optional*: Sesame seeds

Prep Technique:
1. Warm the oven to reach 400° Fahrenheit.
2. Prepare a baking sheet using a layer of parchment baking paper.
3. Toss the mozzarella and cream cheese in a microwave-safe container.
4. Set the timer for one minute and set aside for now.

5. Sift the almond flour, salt, and baking powder in a mixing dish. Whisk and add in one of the eggs. Shred the mozzarella and fold in with the cream cheese.

6. Portion the dough into six balls. Poke your finger in the center and work it to form the bagel shape. Arrange the bagels on a baking sheet.

7. Whisk an egg and gently brush the tops. Leave plain or add your favorite toppings.

8. Bake for approximately 12 to 15 minutes. The tops will have browned to your liking.

9. Serve with a portion of grass-fed butter or cream cheese.

10.   *Note:* As the cheese cools, it may become more difficult to mix. You can microwave the dough for 10 seconds to make it more pliable.

French Toast Bagel

Servings Provided: 6

Cooking & Prep Time: 25-30 min.

Macro Counts For Each Serving:

- **Protein**: 8 g
- **Fat Content**: 16 g
- **Calories**: 207

- **Total Net Carbs**: 3 g

Ingredient List:
- Melted butter (.33 cup)
- Eggs (6)
- Cinnamon (1 tbsp.)
- Maple extract (1 tsp.)
- Sugar-free vanilla extract (2 tsp.)
- Stevia glycerite (5-10 drops) or Swerve sweetener (1 to 1.5 tbsp.)
- Salt (.5 tsp.)
- Sifted coconut flour (.5 cup)
- *Optional:* Xanthan gum or guar gum (.5 tsp.)
- Baking powder (.5 tsp.)

Prep Technique:
1. Warm the oven at 400° Fahrenheit. Lightly grease the pan.
2. Blend the eggs with the cinnamon, vanilla extract, maple extract, stevia, salt, and butter.
3. Whisk the coconut flour with the baking powder and guar/xanthan gum.
4. Combine everything. Spoon into the pan. Bake for 15 minutes.

5. Cool thoroughly and store in a securely closed container.

6. Store in the refrigerator to achieve the best results.

Mozzarella Dough Bagels

Servings Provided: 6

Cooking & Prep Time: 25 min.

Macro Counts For Each Serving:
- **Protein**: 16.8 g
- **Fat Content**: 16.8 g
- **Calories**: 203
- **Total Net Carbs**: 2.4 g

Ingredient List:
- Mozzarella cheese (1.75 cups)
- Salt (1 pinch)
- Almond meal (.75 cup)
- Baking powder (1 tsp.)
- Full-fat cream cheese (2 tbsp.)
- Egg (1 medium)

Prep Technique:

1. Combine the shredded mozzarella cheese with the cream cheese and almond meal in mixing bowl. Cook for one minute.
2. Stir the mixture and continue using the high-temperature setting for another 30 seconds.
3. Whisk the egg, baking powder, salt, and any other flavorings.
4. Portion the dough into six segments. Roll into balls and then into cylinder shapes.
5. Fold the ends together to form the bagels. Be sure to secure the ends of the bagels, so they do not become separated during the cooking process.
6. Arrange the bagels on the baking pan and sprinkle with s few of the sesame seeds.
7. Bake at 425° Fahrenheit until golden brown (about 15 min.).

Onion Bagels

Servings Provided: 6

Cooking & Prep Time: 50-55 min.

Macro Counts For Each Serving:
- **Protein**: 5 g
- **Fat Content**: 5 g
- **Calories**: 78

- **Total Net Carbs**: 1 g

Ingredient List:

- Flaxseed meal (3 tbsp.)
- Coconut flour (2 tbsp.)
- Baking powder (.5 tsp.)
- Eggs (4 separated)
- Dried minced onion (1 tsp.)

Prep Technique:

1. Heat the oven to 325° Fahrenheit.
2. Spray the bagel pan with a spritz of cooking oil.
3. Combine the flax meal with the baking powder, coconut flour, and onion.
4. Mix the egg whites until foamy using an electric mixer.
5. Beat the yolks and combine the fixings.
6. Let the batter rest for about five to ten minutes.
7. Spoon into the donut mold. Sprinkle with additional dried onion to your liking.
8. Bake for 30 minutes. Allow cooling in the oven.

Rosemary Bagels

Servings Provided: 4

Cooking & Prep Time: 55 min.

Macro Counts For Each Serving:

- **Protein**: 13 g
- **Fat Content**: 22.5 g
- **Calories**: 285
- **Total Net Carbs**: 4.5 g

Ingredient List:

- Almond flour (1.5 cups)
- Baking soda (.75 tsp.)
- Xanthan gum (.75 tsp.)
- Salt (.25 tsp.)
- Psyllium husk powder (3 tbsp.)
- Whole egg (1)
- Egg whites (3)
- Warm water (.5 cup)
- Rosemary (1 tbsp. - chopped)
- Avocado oil

Prep Technique:

1. Set the oven temperature at 250° Fahrenheit.

2. Whisk the xanthan gum with the baking soda, almond flour, and salt together in a mixing container.

3. In another dish, whisk eggs and warm water together. Stir in psyllium husk until there are no clumps.

4. Add liquid ingredients to dry ingredients.

5. Coat a bagel mold with avocado oil.

6. Press dough into the mold.

7. Sprinkle rosemary on top.

8. Place in the oven and bake for 45 minutes.

9. Remove and cool for 15 minutes before slicing.

Sesame & Poppy Seed Bagels

Servings Provided: 6

Cooking & Prep Time: 18-25 min.

Macro Counts For Each Serving:

- **Protein**: 20 g
- **Fat Content**: 29 g
- **Calories**: 350
- **Total Net Carbs**: 5 g

Ingredient List:

- Sesame cheese (8 tsp.)

- Poppy seeds (8 tsp.)
- Shredded mozzarella cheese (2.5 cups)
- Baking powder (1 tsp.)
- Almond flour (1.5 cups)
- Large eggs (2)

Prep Technique:

1. Set the oven temperature to 400° Fahrenheit.
2. Prepare a baking sheet with a layer of parchment paper. Combine the almond flour and baking powder.
3. Melt the mozzarella and cream cheese in a micro-safe dish for one minute.
4. Stir and cook one additional minute.
5. Whisk the eggs and add the cheese mixture. Stir and combine with the rest of the fixings. Once the dough is formed, break it apart into six pieces.
6. Stretch the dough and join the ends to form the bagels. Arrange on the baking sheet.
7. Sprinkle with the seed combination and bake for 15 minutes.

Chapter 4: Keto Pizzas

Almond Flour Pizza Crust

Servings Provided: 8

Cooking & Prep Time: 55 min.

Macro Counts For Each Serving:

- **Protein**: 8 g
- **Fat Content**: 14 g
- **Calories**: 182
- **Total Net Carbs**: 3 g

Ingredient List:

- Almond flour (1.5 cups)
- Grated parmesan cheese (.5 cup)
- Flax meal or Whole psyllium husks (1 tbsp.)
- Bak. powder (.5 tsp.)
- Oregano (.5 tsp.)
- Basil (.5 tsp.)
- Garlic powder (.5 tsp.)
- Large eggs (2)
- Water (2 tbsp. or more if needed)
- Olive oil (1 tbsp.)

Prep Technique:

1. Set the oven temperature at 375° Fahrenheit.
2. Whisk the almond flour with the parmesan cheese, basil, oregano, psyllium baking powder, and garlic powder.
3. In another dish, whisk the oil with the water and eggs.
4. Combine everything, adding more water if needed.
5. Shape the dough into a ball. Prepare between two layers of parchment baking paper. Roll it out and transfer to a pizza pan. Discard the top paper.
6. Bake until the crust is browned or about 20-25 minutes. Cool for about 15 minutes.
7. Flip the crust over in the pan. Discard the paper. Add the pizza sauce and chosen toppings.
8. Bake under the oven broiler to melt the cheese and fixings to your liking.

BBQ Chicken Pizza

Servings Provided: 4

Cooking & Prep Time: 25 min.

Macro Counts For Each Serving:
- **Protein**: 24.5 g
- **Fat Content**: 24.5 g

- **Calories**: 357
- **Total Net Carbs**: 2.9 g

Ingredient List - The Crust:

- Eggs (6 large)
- Parmesan cheese (6 tbsp.)
- Psyllium husk powder (3 tbsp.)
- Italian seasoning (1.5 tsp.)
- Salt and pepper (as desired)

Ingredient List - Toppings:

- Cheddar cheese (4 oz.)
- Rotisserie chicken (6 oz. shredded)
- Mayonnaise (1 tbsp.)
- BBQ sauce (4 tbsp.)
- Rao's Tomato Sauce (4 tbsp.)

Prep Technique:

Set the oven at 425° Fahrenheit.

1. Use an immersion blender to combine all of the fixings for the crust until thickened.
2. Spread the dough onto a Silpat using a silicone spatula for shaping. Bake on the top rack for 10 minutes.
3. Flip the pizza over and top with your favorite toppings.
4. Broil for an additional three minutes.

BBQ Meat-Lovers Pizza

Servings Provided: 2

Cooking & Prep Time: 45 min.

Macro Counts For Each Serving:

- **Protein**: 18 g
- **Fat Content**: 27 g
- **Total Net Carbs**: 3.5 g

Ingredient List:

- Mozzarella (2 cups or 8 oz.)
- Psyllium husk powder (1 tbsp.)
- Almond flour (.75 cup)
- Cream cheese (1.5 oz. or 3 tbsp.)

- Large egg (1)
- Black pepper (.5 tsp.)
- Salt (.5 tsp.)
- Italian seasoning (1 tbsp.)

Ingredient List - The Toppings:

- BBQ sauce
- Mozzarella cheese (1 cup)
- Sliced Kabana/hard salami
- Bacon slices
- Sprinkled oregano

Prep Technique:

1. Prepare the temperature of the oven to reach 400º Fahrenheit.
2. Melt the cheese in the microwave – about 45 seconds. Toss in the cream cheese and egg, mixing well.
3. Stir in the psyllium husk along with the flour, salt, pepper, and Italian seasoning. Make the dough as circular as possible. Bake for ten minutes. Flip it onto a sheet of parchment paper.
4. Cover the crust with the toppings. Sprinkle with more cheese.
5. Bake until the cheese is golden.

Bell Pepper Pizza

Servings Provided: 4

Cooking & Prep Time: 25-30 min.

Macro Counts For Each Serving:

- **Protein**: 22.3 g
- **Fat Content**: 31.3 g
- **Calories**: 411.5
- **Total Net Carbs**: 6.5 g

Ingredient List:

- Mozzarella cheese (6 oz.)
- Fresh parmesan cheese (2 tbsp.)
- Cream cheese (2 tbsp.)
- Italian seasoning (1 tsp.)
- Psyllium husk (2 tbsp.)
- Large egg (1)
- Black pepper (.5 tsp.)
- Salt (.5 tsp.)

Ingredient List - The Toppings:

- Shredded cheddar cheese (4 oz.)
- Marinara sauce (.25 cup)
- Medium tomato (1)

- Medium bell peppers (2-3)
- Freshly chopped basil (2 to 3 tbsp.)

Prep Technique:

1. Set the temperature in the oven to 400º Fahrenheit.
2. Melt the cheese in the microwave for 40 to 50 seconds or until pliable. Add the remainder of the pizza base fixings to the cheese and mix well.
3. Shape the dough to form two pizzas.
4. Bake for ten minutes. Remove and add the toppings.
5. Bake for another 8 to 10 minutes.
6. Cool slightly, slice, and serve.

Breakfast Pizza Waffles

Servings Provided: 2

Cooking & Prep Time: 15 min.

Macro Counts For Each Serving:

- **Protein**: 30.65 g
- **Fat Content**: 48.14 g
- **Calories**: 604
- **Total Net Carbs**: 7.59g

Ingredient List:

- Large eggs (4)
- Grated parmesan cheese (4 tbsp.)
- Italian seasoning (1 tsp.)
- Psyllium husk powder (1 tbsp.)
- Almond flour (3 tbsp.)
- Baking powder (1 tsp.)
- Salt and pepper (as desired)
- Bacon grease (1 tbsp.)
- Tomato sauce (.5 cup)
- Cheddar cheese (3 oz.)
- *Optional*: Pepperoni (14 slices)

Prep Technique:

1. Use an immersion blender to prepare all ingredients together until it thickens (except for tomato sauce and cheese).
2. Heat the waffle iron.
3. Prepare the batter in two batches.
4. Add the tomato sauce (.25 cup each) and cheese (1.5 oz. each) onto each waffle.
5. Broil for three to five minutes in the oven. Add pepperoni if desired but count the carbs.

Buffalo Chicken Crust Pizza

Servings Provided: 8

Cooking & Prep Time: 50-55 min.

Macro Counts For Each Serving:

- **Protein**: 13.83 g
- **Fat Content**: 12.88 g
- **Calories**: 172
- **Total Net Carbs**: 0.79 g

Ingredient List:

- Chicken thighs (1 lb.)
- Shredded mozzarella - whole milk (1 cup)
- Large egg (1)
- Dried oregano (1 tsp.)
- Black pepper and salt (.25 tsp. each)
- Butter (2 tbsp.)
- Celery (1 stalk)
- Sour cream (1 tbsp.)
- Franks Red Hot Original (3 tbsp.)
- Blue cheese crumbles (1 oz.)
- Green onion (1 stalk)

Prep Technique:

1. Warm the oven to 400° Fahrenheit. Cut and place a layer of parchment paper onto a pizza pan and set aside for now. Finely dice the celery.
2. Remove all of the bones and skin from the chicken. Grind using the blade attachment on a food processor into a large mixing container.
3. Whisk and add the egg, salt, and .5 cup of shredded mozzarella to the mixing container.
4. Mix the crust until all of the shredded cheese is enclosed in the dough.
5. Spread the chicken out until its .25-inch thick in the pizza pan. Bake until the crust is starting to brown on top (25 min.).
6. Meanwhile, add and melt the butter in a skillet and sauté the celery until it wilts.
7. Blend in 2 tbsp. of hot sauce and the sour cream in a small bowl.
8. Remove the crust and add the sauce layered with the celery, rest of the mozzarella, and crumbles of blue cheese.
9. Bake until the cheese is melted and starts to brown (10 min.). Switch to broil for the last few minutes.
10. Drizzle hot sauce and garnish with green onion slices before serving.

Margherita Keto Pizza

Servings Provided: 6

Cooking & Prep Time: 35-40 min.

Macro Counts For Each Serving:

- **Protein**: 15 g
- **Fat Content**: 17 g
- **Calories**: 237
- **Total Net Carbs**: 4 g

Ingredient List - The Fathead Dough:

- Part-skim shredded mozzarella cheese (1.5 cups)
- Almond flour (.75 cup)
- Cream cheese (2 tbsp.)
- Egg (1)
- Garlic powder (.5 tsp.)
- Dried oregano (rosemary, thyme, etc. (.5 tsp.)
- Salt (.5 tsp.)
- Black pepper (.25 tsp.)

Ingredient List - Keto Pizza Margherita:

- Tomato sauce (.25-.33 cup)
- Fresh mozzarella cut into 4 slices (4 oz.)
- Fresh basil leaves (4+)

- *Optional:* Grated parmesan cheese for garnish
- *Optional:* Sprinkle of dried oregano or other seasonings, for garnish

Prep Technique:

1. Set the oven to 400° Fahrenheit.
2. Add and melt the shredded mozzarella cheese and cream cheese in a non-stick skillet using the medium heat setting, stirring until melted.
3. Transfer to the countertop to rest for 30 seconds.
4. Stir in almond flour, egg, garlic powder, dried seasonings, salt, and pepper; continue to stir until thoroughly combined.
5. Transfer the dough to a parchment paper-lined surface.
6. Add another piece of parchment paper over the dough. Take a rolling pin and place over the top parchment paper; start rolling into a circle until the dough is thin and spread out to about nine inches.
7. If you do not have a rolling pin, wet the palms of your hands with cooking spray and press out the dough into a thin round.

8. Remove the top parchment paper and slide the dough onto a baking sheet leaving the bottom paper attached.
9. Use a fork and dot the dough before adding it into the oven for 10 minutes.
10.   If you see any bubbles forming on top of the pizza crust, remove the pie from the oven, poke down with a fork, and continue to bake.
11.   When the crust is finished cooking, let stand for a minute.

Prep Technique - The Keto Pizza:

1. Spread a thin layer of tomato sauce over the pizza crust and top with mozzarella cheese.
2. Bake for an additional 7 to 8 minutes, or until cheese is melted and pizza is bubbly.
3. Remove from the oven, top with fresh basil leaves, sprinkle with parmesan cheese, and oregano to serve.
4. *Note:* To prevent a 'scrambled egg' effect, let the cheese cool for a bit before stirring in the egg.

Pepperoni Pizza

Servings Provided: 6

Cooking & Prep Time: 25-30 min.

Macro Counts For Each Serving:

- **Protein**: 18.2 g
- **Fat Content**: 27 g
- **Calories**: 335
- **Total Net Carbs**: 3.2 g

Ingredient List - The Base:

- Mozzarella cheese (2 cups/8 oz.)
- Almond flour (.75 cup)
- Psyllium husk powder (1 tbsp.)
- Cream cheese (3 tbsp./1.5 oz.)
- Large egg (1)
- Italian seasoning (1 tbsp.)
- Pepper & Salt (.5 tsp. each)

Ingredient List - Toppings:

- Mozzarella cheese (1 cup/4 oz.)
- Rao's Tomato Sauce (.5 cup)
- Pepperoni (16 slices)
- *Optional*: Sprinkled oregano

Prep Technique:

1. Warm the oven to 400° Fahrenheit.

2. Microwave the mozzarella cheese until completely melted. Add all other base fixings (omit the olive oil) and mix well.
3. Knead the dough into a ball, and spread it out into a circle.
4. Bake the crust for 10 minutes. Remove from the oven, flip, and bake for two to four additional minutes.
5. Toss the crust with toppings of your choice and bake for another three to five minutes.
6. Let cool slightly, slice, and serve!

Pizza Bites

Servings Provided: 4
Cooking & Prep Time: 10-15 min.
Macro Counts For Each Serving:
- **Protein**: 5 g
- **Fat Content**: 7 g
- **Calories**: 94
- **Total Net Carbs**: 2.8 g

Ingredient List:
- Salami (4 slices)
- Marinara sauce (.25 cup)

- Shredded mozzarella (.25 cup)

Prep Technique:

1. Warm up the oven broiler using the high-temperature setting.
2. Add the salami on a baking sheet. Sprinkle with the sauce and cheese.
3. Prepare in the oven for five minutes. Drain the grease on a paper towel for 1 to 2 minutes. Serve. You can add these to a prepared crust.

Pocket Pizza

Servings Provided: 4

Cooking & Prep Time: 20-25 min.

Macro Counts For Each Serving:

- **Protein**: 15.6 g
- **Fat Content**: 24.5 g
- **Calories**: 293
- **Total Net Carbs**: 3.9 g

Ingredient List:

- Pre-shredded/grated cheese mozzarella (1.75 cups)
- Almond flour (.75 cup)

- Full-fat cream cheese (2 tbsp.)
- Egg (1 medium)
- Salt (1 pinch or to taste)

Prep Technique:

1. Mix the shredded cheese, cream cheese, and almond flour in a microwaveable bowl. Microwave using the high power setting for one minute.
2. Stir and continue cooking on high for another 30 seconds.
3. Whisk the egg and salt and mix gently with the rest of the fixings.
4. Roll the dough between two sheets of baking paper.
5. Discard the top baking paper. Slice the dough into squares that are the same size as your toasted sandwich maker.
6. Place one square on the bottom of the sandwich maker; add your choice of fillings.
7. Arrange another square of dough on the top and press the lid of the sandwich maker down.
8. Cook until they're golden brown or about three to five minutes.

Sausage Crust Pizza

Servings Provided: 4

Cooking & Prep Time: 45-55 min.

Macro Counts For Each Serving:

- **Protein**: 31.3 g
- **Fat Content**: 21.2 g
- **Calories**: 357
- **Total Net Carbs**: 12 g

Ingredient List:

- Garlic powder (1 tsp.)
- Onion powder (1 tsp.)
- Italian seasoning (1 tsp.)
- Sausage (1 lb.)
- Diced onion (.5 of 1 small)
- Diced red bell pepper (1)
- Sautéed mushrooms (3 oz.)
- Tomato paste (1 tbsp.)
- Mozzarella cheese (3 oz.)
- Sliced ham (2 oz.)

Prep Technique:

1. Warm the oven until it reaches 350º Fahrenheit.

2. Break the sausage apart and smash onto the sides and bottom of the pan.

3. Once loaded, arrange the pan in the heated oven.

4. Bake for 10 to 15 minutes. Transfer it to a platter when done.

5. Combine the garlic powder, tomato paste, Italian seasoning, onion powder, and garlic powder. Sprinkle over the crust.

6. To prepare, just layer with the ham, onions, mushrooms, and red pepper. Give it a sprinkle of the mozzarella cheese.

7. Cook for 12 to 15 minutes until golden and the cheese is melted.

8. Store the prepared pizza in the refrigerator for a couple of days, but no longer. It is best to freeze as soon as it is cooled.

Thai Chicken Flatbread Pizza

Servings Provided: 12

Cooking & Prep Time: 40-45 min.

Macro Counts For Each Serving:

- **Protein**: 15 g
- **Fat Content**: 21 g
- **Calories**: 268

- **Total Net Carbs**: 3.2 g

Ingredient List - The Sauce:

- PBFit (4 tbsp.)
- Rice wine vinegar (2 tbsp.)
- Fish sauce (1 tsp.)
- Soy sauce (4 tbsp.)
- Reduced-sugar ketchup (4 tbsp.)
- Coconut oil (4 tbsp.)
- Lime juice (.5 of 1 lime)

Ingredient List - The Base:

- Onion powder (.5 tsp.)
- Ginger powder (.5 tsp.)
- Garlic powder (.5 tsp.)
- Mozzarella cheese (2 cups/8 oz.)
- Psyllium husk powder (1 tbsp.)
- Almond flour (.75 cup)
- Salt (.5 tsp.)
- Pepper (.5 tsp.)
- Cream cheese (3 tbsp./1.5 oz.)
- Egg (1 large)

Ingredient List - The Toppings:

- Mozzarella cheese (6 oz.)

- Mung bean sprouts (3 oz.)
- Green onions (2 medium)
- Shredded carrots (1.5 oz.)

- Peanuts (2 tbsp. chopped)
- Cilantro (3 tbsp. chopped)
- Chicken thighs (2 small - cooked)

Prep Technique

1. Set the oven temperature at 400° Fahrenheit.
2. Mix all of the sauce fixings and set to the side for now. Shred the carrots.
3. Microwave the cream cheese and mozzarella for the pizza base for one minute. Mix in the egg and blend with the dry fixings.
4. Spread the dough onto a Silpat (edge to edge). Bake for 11 to 14 minutes.
5. Flip the pizza and top using the prepared sauce, chopped chicken, carrots, and mozzarella.
6. Bake until cheese has melted (7-10 min.).
7. Top with spring onion, bean sprouts, peanuts, and cilantro to your liking.

Zucchini Pizza Bites

Servings Provided: 4

Cooking & Prep Time: 25 min.

Macro Counts For Each Serving:

- **Protein**: 26 g
- **Fat Content**: 43 g
- **Calories**: 505
- **Total Net Carbs**: 2 g

Ingredient List:

- Large zucchini (3-4)
- Pizza sauce - no-sugar-added (.5 cup)
- Sliced pepperoni (12 oz.)
- Shredded mozzarella (1 cup)
- Black pepper & salt (to your liking)

Prep Technique:

1. Heat up the oven to 350º Fahrenheit.
2. Slice the zucchini into .5-inch thick rounds. Sprinkle with salt and pepper. Arrange on a baking sheet.
3. Spoon equal portions of sauce on the rounds with a pinch or two of mozzarella cheese.
4. Garnish with the pepperoni and bake for 15-20 minutes.

Flatbread & Pita Bread Options

Cheese Flatbread

Servings Provided: 6

Cooking & Prep Time: 45 min.

Macro Counts For Each Serving:

- **Protein**: 12.3 g
- **Fat Content**: 11.3 g
- **Calories**: 170
- **Total Net Carbs**: 5 g

Ingredient List:

- Warm buttermilk (1 cup)
- Sifted almond flour (2 cups)
- Grated hard cheese (5.5 oz.)
- Baking powder (.5 tsp.)
- Salt (1 pinch)

Prep Technique:

1. Warm the oven to reach 350º Fahrenheit.
2. Mix the buttermilk with the salt and baking powder.
3. Grate the cheese and combine with the flour. Mix all of the fixings and knead.

4. Make five balls and add them to a parchment paper-lined tray.
5. Flatten into five flatbreads and bake 15 minutes.
6. Flip once and cook five more minutes. Serve hot.

Matzo Bread - Jewish Flatbread

Servings Provided: 6

Cooking & Prep Time: 8-10 min.

Macro Counts For Each Serving:
- **Protein**: 1 g
- **Fat Content**: 2.2 g
- **Calories**: 28
- **Total Net Carbs**: 1g

Ingredient List:
- Sifted almond flour (1 cup)
- Water (.5 cup)
- Salt (1 pinch)

Prep Technique:
1. Warm the oven ahead of cooking time to 475º Fahrenheit.

2. Sift the flour into a mixing container. Blend in water (1 tbsp. at a time). Sprinkle in the salt and knead. Divide into four balls.

3. Prepare a baking tin and add the rolled balls of dough. Flatten into disks and pierce each one to prevent rising.

4. Bake for two minutes per side.

Pita Pizza

Servings Provided: 2

Cooking & Prep Time: 10-15 min.

Macro Counts For Each Serving:

- **Protein**: 13 g
- **Fat Content**: 19 g
- **Calories**: 250
- **Total Net Carbs**: 4g

Ingredient List:

- Marinara sauce (.5 cup)
- Low-carb pita (1)
- Cheddar cheese (2 oz.)
- Pepperoni (14 slices)
- Roasted red peppers (1 oz.)
- Spritz of olive oil

Prep Technique:

1. Set the oven temperature at 450º Fahrenheit.

2. Slice the pita in half. Arrange it on a foil-lined baking tray and spritz with oil. Toast for 1-2 minutes.

3. Empty the sauce over the prepared crust. Dust with the cheddar cheese and rest of the toppings.

4. Bake until the cheese melts or about five minutes.

Chapter 5: Keto Chips - Crackers & Breadsticks

Cheddar Parmesan Chips

Servings Provided: 4

Cooking & Prep Time: 15 min.

Macro Counts For Each Serving:

- **Protein**: 11 g
- **Fat Content**: 11 g
- **Calories**: 152
- **Total Net Carbs**: 1 g

Ingredient List:

- Italian seasoning (1 tsp.)
- Shredded cheddar cheese (.75 cup)
- Parmesan cheese (.75 cup)

Prep Technique:

1. Set the oven temperature to 400º Fahrenheit. Cover a baking tin with a piece of parchment paper.

2. Combine the two kinds of cheese. Arrange on the baking pan approximately two inches apart. Sprinkle with the seasoning.

3. Bake until the edges are browned or about 6-8 minutes.

4. When browned, cool slightly before moving them to a towel to drain.

Tortilla Chips

Servings Provided: 7

Cooking & Prep Time: 25 min.

Macro Counts For Each Serving:

- **Protein**: 10 g
- **Fat Content**: 18 g
- **Calories**: 220
- **Total Net Carbs**: 4 g

Ingredient List:

- Almond flour (2 cups)
- Egg (1 large)
- Garlic powder (.5 tsp.)
- Chili powder (.5 tsp.)
- Cumin (.5 tsp.)
- Sea salt (.25 tsp.)

- Paprika (.25 tsp.)
- Shredded mozzarella cheese (.5 cup)

Prep Technique:

1. Set the oven temperature at 350º Fahrenheit.
2. Arrange parchment baking paper on a baking tin.
3. Combine the spices and flour in a mixing container. Mix in the egg using a hand mixer to form crumbly dough.
4. Microwave the mozzarella until it's easy to stir or melt it in a double boiler on the stovetop.
5. Combine the fixings and knead with your hands. Arrange it between two sheets of parchment paper. Roll it out thinly using a rolling pin.
6. Slice into triangles and place on the prepared baking tin.
7. Bake 8 to 12 minutes or until firm and golden. If there is any extra 'sizzle' splatter, just wipe it away with a towel.
8. They become crispy as they cool.

Crackers

Almond Crackers

Servings Provided: 40 - 10 per serving

Cooking & Prep Time: 34-42 min.

Macro Counts For Each Serving:

- **Protein**: 6 g
- **Fat Content**: 15 g
- **Calories**: 173
- **Total Net Carbs**: 3 g

Ingredient List:

- Almond flour (1 cup)
- Water (3 tbsp.)
- Ground flaxseed (1 tbsp.)
- Fine sea salt (.5 tsp.)
- *Optional:* Flaked sea salt

Prep Technique:

1. Warm the oven to reach 350° Fahrenheit.
2. Prepare the dough by combining the first 4 ingredients. Lay it out on a sheet of parchment paper and cover with a second sheet. Flatten the

dough. You can use your hands or a rolling pin, but press the dough into a 1/8-inch thickness.

3. Sprinkle using the flaked sea salt. Use a pizza slicer to make the cuts about .5-1-inch sections. Try to use triangular cuts.

4. Arrange on a paper-lined baking pan to bake for 20-25 minutes. Cool completely and enjoy any time. Store in an airtight container.

Buttery Pesto Crackers

Servings Provided: 6

Cooking & Prep Time: 26-30 min.

Macro Counts For Each Serving:

- **Protein**: 5.34 g
- **Fat Content**: 19.3 g
- **Calories**: 204.5
- **Total Net Carbs**: 2.96 g

Ingredient List:

- Almond flour (1.25 cups)
- Ground black pepper (.25 tsp.)
- Salt (.5 tsp.)
- Baking powder (.5 tsp.)
- Dried basil (.25 tsp.)

- Cayenne pepper (1 pinch)
- Pressed clove of garlic (1)
- Basil pesto (2 tbsp.)
- Butter (3 tbsp.)

Prep Technique:
1. Warm up the oven to reach 325° Fahrenheit.
2. Line a cookie sheet with a sheet of parchment paper.
3. Prepare the garlic with the press
4. Whisk the baking powder, salt, flour, and pepper.
5. Toss in the cayenne, garlic, and basil. Stir in the pesto and form a dough mixture.
6. Fold in the butter with your fingers or a fork until a dough ball is formed. Arrange on the baking sheet. Spread it out until thin.
7. Bake for 14 to 17 minutes. Remove from the oven. Cool thoroughly before cutting into crackers.

Chia Seed Crackers

Servings Provided: 36

Cooking & Prep Time: 65 min.

Macro Counts For Each Serving:

- **Protein**: 0.88 g
- **Fat Content**: 2.15 g
- **Calories**: 28
- **Total Net Carbs**: 0.28 g

Ingredient List:

- Ground chia seeds (.5 cup)
- Shredded cheddar cheese (3 oz.)
- Ice water (1.25 cups)
- Psyllium husk powder (2 tbsp.)
- Olive oil (2 tbsp.)
- Xanthan gum (.25 tsp.)
- Garlic powder (.25 tsp.)
- Onion powder (.25 tsp.)
- Oregano (.25 tsp.)
- Paprika (.25 tsp.)
- Salt (.25 tsp.)
- Pepper (.25 tsp.)

Prep Technique:

1. Use a spice grinder to prepare the chia seeds and add to the rest of the dry fixings. Warm up the oven to reach 375° Fahrenheit.

2. Blend the oil into the dry components to make a sandy consistency. Add the water into the mixture to form the dough.

3. Fold in the cheddar and mix well. Place on a Silpat to rest 5 minutes or so. Roll out the dough until it's 'super' thin.

4. Bake for 30 to 35 minutes. Remove and slice into individual crackers.

5. Place back in the oven to broil for 5 to 7 minutes until crispy.

6. Chill and serve or store.

Graham Crackers

Servings Provided: 24

Cooking & Prep Time: 45 min.

Macro Counts For Each Serving:

- **Protein**: 4 g
- **Fat Content**: 12 g
- **Calories**: 135
- **Total Net Carbs**: 2 g

Ingredient List:

- Melted butter (6 tbsp.)
- Chopped pistachios (.5 cup)

- Erythritol (.5 cup)
- Almond flour (2 cups)

Prep Technique:

1. Mix each of the fixings together in a mixing container.
2. Shape the dough into a long roll and cover with a sheet of plastic wrap.
3. Place in the fridge for about ½ hour. Unwrap and slice into 16 portions.
4. Bake for 12 to 15 minutes.

Healthy Goat Cheese Crackers

Servings Provided: 12

Cooking & Prep Time: 30 min.

Macro Counts For Each Serving:

- **Protein**: 3 g
- **Fat Content**: 8 g
- **Calories**: 99
- **Total Net Carbs**: 2 g

Ingredient List:

- Baking powder (1 tsp.)
- Fresh rosemary (2 tbsp.)

- Butter (4 tbsp.)
- Coconut flour (.5 cup)
- Goat cheese (6 oz.)

Prep Technique:

1. Set the oven to 380° Fahrenheit.
2. Use a food processor to mix all of the components, processing until creamy smooth.
3. Roll the dough out using a rolling pin until it's about .25-.5-inches thick. Use a cookie cutter or knife to portion the crackers.
4. Place on a paper-lined pan.
5. Bake for 15-20 minutes.

Hemp Heart Crackers

Servings Provided: 36

Cooking & Prep Time: 1 hr. 10 min.

Macro Counts For Each Serving:

- **Protein**: 1 g
- **Fat Content**: 6 g
- **Calories**: 76
- **Total Net Carbs**: 1 g

Ingredient List:

- Almond flour (1 cup)
- Coconut flour (.5 cup (+) more for preparing the dough)
- Hemp hearts (.5 cup)
- Baking powder (3 tsp.)
- Optional: Xanthan gum (1 tsp.)
- Salt for topping (.5 tsp.)
- Baking soda (.25 tsp.)
- Salted butter – very cold (6 tbsp.)
- Melted butter with salt (4 tbsp.)
- Olive oil (2 tbsp.)
- Ice water (.66 cup)

Prep Technique:
1. Warm the oven to 400° Fahrenheit.
2. Put the hemp hearts, almond flour, baking soda, coconut flour, baking powder, and salt in a mixing container – mixing well.
3. Grate the chilled butter, stirring it into the flour mixture.
4. Pour in the olive oil. Stir until all of the olive oil is blended into the flour mixture and add the water.
5. Place the dough in the fridge for at least 30 minutes.

6. At that time, dust a Silpat or sheet of parchment with coconut flour.

7. Prepare the dough (1/4-inch thickness), and dust with flour. Cut into the desired shapes.

8. You can use a toothpick to poke holes in the crackers. Bake for 15 to 20 minutes.

9. Prepare the butter with .5 tsp. of salt to brush the crackers while they are hot.

10.   For best results, turn off the oven off. Put the tray back in the oven for about five minutes for a crispier cracker.

11.   Remove and cool the batch entirely before storing.

Rosemary & Sea Salt Flax Crackers

Servings Provided: Varies 17-20

Cooking & Prep Time: 25-30 min.

Macro Counts For Each Serving:

- **Protein**: 10 g
- **Fat Content**: 10 g
- **Calories**: 110
- **Total Net Carbs**: 2 g

Ingredient List:

- Ground/milled flax seeds (1 cup)
- Eggs (2)
- Grated romano/parmesan cheese (.5 cup)
- Freshly minced rosemary (1 tsp.)
- Sea salt (as desired)

Prep Technique:

1. Warm the oven to 350° Fahrenheit.
2. Spray a cookie sheet (or two) with a spritz of cooking oil spray.
3. Add all of the fixings (omit the salt) into a mixing container, stirring until fully mixed. Let the mixture rest for about five minutes.
4. Prepare a cutting board and rolling pin with a spritz of cooking oil spray.
5. Form the dough into a ball and roll it out as thin as desired.
6. Use a cookie cutter to cut a grid of one-inch squares.
7. Transfer the individual crackers onto the pan.
8. Sprinkle with salt and bake for 10 minutes, remove and flip. Bake another three minutes.

Salty Butter Crackers

Servings Provided: 25

Cooking & Prep Time: 35 min.

Macro Counts For Each Serving:

- **Protein**: 2 g
- **Fat Content**: 8 g
- **Calories**: 90
- **Total Net Carbs**: 1 g

Ingredient List:

- Almond flour (2.25 cups)
- Egg whites (2)
- Softened - not melted – salted butter (8 tbsp.)
- Salt (1 pinch or as desired)

Prep Technique:

1. Warm the oven temperature to 350° Fahrenheit.
2. Combine the butter and egg whites in a mixing container on the low-medium setting using a hand mixer until smooth.
3. Fold in the salt and almond flour – mixing a low speed until well mixed.

4. Arrange the dough between two sheets of parchment baking paper. Roll out the dough on the baking tin.

5. Score the crackers lightly using a pizza cutter or sharp knife into approximately 1.5-inch squares.

6. Bake for 10-15 minutes. Cool and gently break apart on the scored lines.

7. *Note*: Cool fully before slicing.

Super-Easy TJ Keto Crackers

Servings Provided: 18 crackers

Cooking & Prep Time: 13-14 min. - varies

Macro Counts For Each Serving:

- **Protein**: 1.2 g
- **Fat Content**: 4.3 g
- **Calories**: 46
- **Total Net Carbs**: 0.5 g

Ingredient List:

- Salted grass-fed butter (2.5 tbsp.)
- Almond flour (1 cup)
- Xanthan gum (.5 tsp.)
- Baking powder (.25 tsp.)

- Kosher salt (1 pinch - if using unsalted butter - up the salt to .25 tsp.)
- Egg (1.5 tbsp.)
- TJ's Everything But The Bagel Seasoning

Prep Technique:

1. Melt butter in a small microwave-safe container until just melted. Set aside to cool while you mix each of the flours.
2. Whisk the almond flour, baking powder, xanthan gum, and salt.
3. Pour in the butter and mix until evenly distributed. Add in a lightly whisked egg (1.5 tbsp.) and continue to knead until it forms into a ball. Cover in a cling film such as Saran Wrap, and place in the freezer for about five minutes to solidify the batter.
4. Roll out the dough between two sheets of parchment paper. Sprinkle using the seasoning and lightly roll again to press it in.
5. Trim to desired cracker size and separate gently using a butter knife.
6. For medium crackers, cook on high in the parchment paper for 20 seconds, open the

microwave and cook for another 15 to 20 seconds.

7. Note: The crackers will continue to crisp up as they cool.

Toasted Sesame Crackers

Servings Provided: 6

Cooking & Prep Time: 30 min.

Macro Counts For Each Serving:

- **Protein**: 11 g
- **Fat Content**: 17 g
- **Calories**: 213
- **Total Net Carbs**: 3 g

Ingredient List:

- Toasted sesame seeds (.25 cup)
- Almond flour (1 cup)
- Grated Asiago cheese (.5 cup)
- Egg white (1)
- Dijon mustard (1 tbsp.)
- Salt (.5 tsp.)
- Paprika (1 tsp.)

Prep Technique:

1. Warm the oven until it reaches 325° Fahrenheit.
2. Lightly grease a sheet of foil in a baking pan.
3. Combine each of the fixings except for the salt into the processor. Blend until it shapes into dough.
4. Take it from the processor and roll out the dough to form a log. Slice them into .25-inch slices.
5. Arrange on a baking sheet and sprinkle with the salt.
6. Bake for 17 to 20 minutes.

Breadsticks

Cheesy Garlic Breadstick Bites

Servings Provided: 7

Cooking & Prep Time: 30-35 min.

Macro Counts For Each Serving:

- **Protein**: 5.4 g
- **Fat Content**: 4.18 g
- **Calories**: 135.2
- **Total Net Carbs**: 2.36 g

Ingredient List:

- Shredded cheddar cheese (.25 cup)

- Cream cheese - softened (2 oz.)
- Almond flour (.5 cup)
- Dried chives (1 tsp.)
- Coconut flour (1 tbsp.)
- Minced garlic (1 tsp.)
- Slightly beaten egg white (1)

Prep Technique:

1. Warm the oven to reach 350º Fahrenheit.
2. Prepare a baking tin with a layer of paper.
3. Combine the cheddar and cream cheese in a mixing container.
4. Stir in the minced garlic, chives, almond and coconut flour, and egg white. It should not be crumbly or dry, but soft.
5. Add the mixture to a plastic bag. Snip away about a 1-inch corner, or use a pastry bag to pipe the dough onto the baking pan.
6. Make 3-inch strips with the prepared dough. Flatten each one with the tongs of a fork.
7. Bake for 10 to 15 minutes. Serve.

Coconut & Flax Breadsticks

Servings Provided: 5/20 sticks

Cooking & Prep Time: 60-65 min.

Macro Counts For Each Serving:

- **Protein**: 13 g
- **Fat Content**: 27 g
- **Calories**: 334
- **Total Net Carbs**: 4.2 g

Ingredient List:

- Flax meal/ground flaxseed (.75 cup)
- Almond flour (1 cup)
- Salt (1 tsp.)
- Coconut flour (.25 cup)
- Chia seeds (2 tbsp.)
- Psyllium husk powder (1 tbsp.)
- Lukewarm water (1 cup (+) 2 tbsp. if the dough is dry)

Ingredient List- Toppings:

- Mixed seeds - ex. Poppyseed, sesame, or caraway (4 tbsp.)
- Egg yolks (2 large - For egg-free use water or melted ghee)
- Coarse sea salt - Pink Himalayan (1 tsp.)

Ingredient List - Optional Garnishes:

- Marinara sauce
- BBQ sauce
- Keto Cheese sauce
- Pesto

Prep Technique:

1. Warm up the oven to reach 350° Fahrenheit.
2. Combine all of the ingredients to form dough. Work it until it holds together and set it aside for 15-20 minutes.
3. Divide the dough into four segments. Then, into five pieces. Form the stick about ten inches long.
4. Put the breadsticks on a paper-lined baking tin, and brush with the yolks or ghee.
5. Give them a sprinkle of salt, seeds, and parmesan cheese. Turn up the oven to 360° Fahrenheit.
6. Bake for 15-20 minutes until crispy.

Italian Breadsticks

Servings Provided: 16

Cooking & Prep Time: 30-34 min.

Macro Counts For Each Serving:

- **Protein**: 8 g
- **Fat Content**: 10 g

- **Calories**: 130
- **Total Net Carbs**: 2 g

Ingredient List:

- Almond flour (1.5 cups)
- Psyllium husk powder (1 tbsp.)
- Baking powder (2 tsp.)
- Nutritional yeast (1 tbsp.)
- Garlic salt (1 tsp.)
- Dried parsley (2 tsp.)
- Dried basil (.5 tsp.)
- Shredded mozzarella cheese (2.5 cups)
- Cream cheese (3 oz.)
- Eggs (2)
- Grated parmesan cheese (2 tbsp.)
- Garlic cloves (2)
- Flavorless oil - as needed for prep
- Olive oil for brushing the tops

Prep Technique:

1. Warm the oven before baking time to reach 400° Fahrenheit.
2. Line the baking tray.
3. Prepare the garlic cloves with a press.

4. Place the mozzarella and cream cheese into the bowl. Cook for one minute.

5. Add and whisk the almond flour, nutritional yeast, psyllium husk powder, oregano, parsley, basil, garlic salt, and baking powder in a separate bowl.

6. Add the eggs in with the mozzarella, fresh garlic, and cream cheese.

7. Combine and add in the parmesan, then add in the dry fixings.

8. Divide the dough into eight pieces. Shape into logs and divide into sixteen breadsticks total.

9. Arrange them on a layer of parchment baking paper and place on the top oven rack. Be sure to rotate the breadsticks about halfway through the baking cycle to ensure its cooking evenly.

10. Bake for 12 minutes.

11. When the time is up, transfer to the countertop and lightly brush olive oil over the tops.

12. Bake for an additional three minutes.

13. Cool slightly before serving.

Oat Sticks

Servings Provided: 8

Cooking & Prep Time: 17-25 min.

Macro Counts For Each Serving:

- **Protein**: 4 g
- **Fat Content**: 10.2 g
- **Calories**: 137
- **Total Net Carbs**: 7.5 g

Ingredient List:

- Finely ground oat flakes (1 cup)
- Almond flour (.5 cup)
- Salt (1 pinch)
- Grated cheese - your preference (2 oz.)
- Cubed butter (2.5 oz.)
- Almond milk (1 cup)

Prep Technique:

1. Line a baking tin with paper.
2. Warm up the oven to 375° Fahrenheit.
3. Sift the flour. Add the salt and oat flakes.
4. Fold in the cubed butter, grated cheese, and milk.
5. Knead the dough and roll out to a 1/4-inch thickness using a rolling pin. Slice into sticks.
6. Bake until lightly browned or about 12 minutes. Watch the sticks carefully starting at the 10-minute marker.

3-Way Tasty Breadsticks

Servings Provided: 6

Cooking & Prep Time: 25-30 min.

Ingredient List - The Base:

- Mozzarella cheese (2 cups - 8 oz.)
- Almond flour (.75 cup)
- Psyllium husk powder (1 tbsp.)
- Cream cheese (1.5 oz. - 3 tbsp.)
- Large egg (1)
- Baking powder (1 tsp.)

Choice 1: Extra Cheesy Breadsticks

Macro Counts For Each Serving:

- **Protein**: 18 g
- **Fat Content**: 25 g
- **Calories**: 314
- **Total Net Carbs**: 3.6 g

Ingredient List - Cheesy:

- Garlic powder (1 tsp.)
- Onion powder (1 tsp.)
- Cheddar cheese (3 oz.)
- Parmesan cheese (.25 cup)

Choice 2: Italian Style Breadsticks

Macro Counts For Each Serving:

- **Protein**: 12.8 g
- **Fat Content**: 18.8 g
- **Calories**: 238
- **Total Net Carbs**: 2.6 g

Ingredient List - Italian:

- Italian seasoning (2 tbsp.)
- Salt & Pepper (1 tsp. each)

Choice 3: Cinnamon Sugar

Macro Counts For Each Serving:

- **Protein**: 13 g
- **Fat Content**: 24.3 g
- **Calories**: 292
- **Total Net Carbs**: 3.3 g

Ingredient List - Cinnamon Sugar:

- Butter (3 tbsp.)
- Swerve sweetener (6 tbsp.)
- Cinnamon (2 tbsp.)

Prep Technique:

1. For any of the types of breadsticks; just warm up the oven to 400° Fahrenheit.

2. Combine the cream cheese and egg until just mixed.

3. In another container, mix each of the dry fixings.

4. Portion the cheese into a microwavable dish and cook at 20-second intervals until sizzling hot. Stir in the cream cheese, eggs, and dry fixings.

5. Knead the dough and press flat using a Silpat. Transfer to a piece of foil and slice into pizza forms you like.

6. Bake the pieces for 13-15 minutes on the top rack until crispy. Serve warm.

Chapter 6: Keto Muffin Specialties

Sweet Options

Apple Almond Muffins

Servings Provided: 12

Cooking & Prep Time: 25 min.

Macro Counts For Each Serving:

- **Protein**: 5 g
- **Fat Content**: 15 g
- **Calories**: 184
- **Total Net Carbs**: 10 g

Ingredient List:

- Almond flour (2.5 cups)

- Cinnamon (1 tsp.)
- Eggs (2)
- Melted butter (.33 cup)
- Maple syrup (4 tbsp.)
- Thinly sliced apple (1)

Prep Technique:

1. Warm up the oven to 350° Fahrenheit.
2. Mix all of the fixings – omitting the apple.
3. Peel and fold the apple slices and pour the dough into the cups.
4. Bake for 15 minutes. Cool before storing.

Applesauce - Cinnamon & Nutmeg Muffins

Servings Provided: 12

Cooking & Prep Time: 30 min.

Macro Counts For Each Serving:

- **Protein**: 7 g
- **Fat Content**: 22 g
- **Calories**: 241
- **Total Net Carbs**: 3 g

Ingredient List:

- Melted ghee (.5 cup)

- Large whisked eggs (3)
- Nutmeg (1 tsp.)
- Cinnamon (3 tbsp.)
- Almond flour (3 cups)
- Cloves (.25 tsp.)
- Applesauce (4 tbsp.)
- Baking powder (1 tsp.)
- Stevia (to taste)
- Lemon juice (1 tsp.)

Prep Technique:

1. Set the oven temperature to 350º Fahrenheit.
2. Combine the ingredients in a mixing container.
3. Empty the batter into the muffin pan.
4. Bake for about 17 to 20 minutes until the center is springy.
5. Cool before storing.

Banana & Applesauce Muffins

Servings Provided: 12

Cooking & Prep Time: 35-40 min.

Macro Counts For Each Serving:

- **Protein**: 11 g
- **Fat Content**: 4 g

- **Calories**: 134
- **Total Net Carbs**: 8 g

Ingredient List:

- Baking powder (1 tsp.)
- Whole wheat flour (1.33 cups)
- Salt (.25 tsp.)
- Baking soda (.5 tsp.)
- Egg (1)
- Olive oil (3 tbsp.)
- Unsweetened applesauce (.5 cup)
- Vanilla extract (1 tsp.)
- Ripe bananas (1.5 cups)

Prep Technique:

1. Heat the oven to reach 375º Fahrenheit. Heavily grease a muffin tin.
2. Whisk the egg and add the mashed bananas. Stir in everything but the flour.
3. Next, using caution, not to over mix, fold in the flour.
4. Pour a portion of the batter into each of the tins.
5. Bake for approximately 20-25 minutes.

6. When the muffins are done, transfer them to the countertop, and cool in the pan for about 5 minutes.
7. Cool thoroughly before storing.

Blackberry Lemon Muffins

Servings Provided: 12

Cooking & Prep Time: 42-45 min.

Macro Counts For Each Serving:
- **Protein**: 8 g
- **Fat Content**: 25 g
- **Calories**: 277
- **Total Net Carbs**: 5 g

Ingredient List:
- Almond flour (2 cups)
- Sea salt (.125 tsp.)
- GF baking powder (2 tsp.)
- Coconut flour (1 tbsp.)
- Heavy cream (.5 cup)
- Large eggs - room temperature (2)
- Melted butter (.25 cup)
- Lemon juice (1 tbsp.) & zest (1 lemon)
- Pure vanilla extract (1 tsp.)

- Liquid stevia (12 drops)
- Fresh firm blackberries or cherries - fresh or frozen (1.5 cups)
- Chopped pecans (.5 cup)

Prep Technique:

1. Heat the oven to reach 350° Fahrenheit.
2. Prepare a muffin pan with paper liners.
3. Mix the baking powder, almond flour, and salt into a food processor.
4. Pour in the cream, eggs, lemon juice, butter, lemon zest, vanilla, and stevia. Blend until creamy.
5. Fold in the blackberries and pecans.
6. Empty the mixture into the muffin tins.
7. Bake for 30 to 35 minutes. Cool in the pan before removing.
8. *Notes*: If you don't have a food processor use an electric mixer.
9. If you are using frozen berries, don't defrost before adding to the recipe.

Blueberry Cream Cheese Muffins

Servings Provided: 12

Cooking & Prep Time: 30 min.

Macro Counts For Each Serving:

- **Protein**: 3 g
- **Fat Content**: 14 g
- **Calories**: 155
- **Total Net Carbs**: 2 g

Ingredient List:

- Softened unchilled cream cheese (16 oz.)
- Low-carb sweetener (.5 cup)
- Eggs (2)
- Xanthan gum optional (.25 tsp.)
- Sugar-free vanilla extract (.5 tsp.)
- Blueberries (.25 cup)
- Sliced almonds (.25 cup)
- *Also Needed*: 12-count muffin molds with paper liners

Prep Technique:

1. Warm up the oven to 350° Fahrenheit.
2. Blend the cheese until it's a creamy texture.
3. Stir in the eggs, sweetener, vanilla, and xanthan gum.
4. Blend well. Stir in the blueberries and almonds.

5. Scoop into the molds and bake for about 20 minutes.
6. Chill and serve.

Brownie Muffins

Servings Provided: 6

Cooking & Prep Time: 20-25 min.

Macro Counts For Each Serving:

- **Protein**: 7 g
- **Fat Content**: 13 g
- **Calories**: 183
- **Total Net Carbs**: 4.4 g

Ingredient List:

- Salt (.5 tsp.)
- Flaxseed meal (1 cup)
- Cocoa powder (.25 cup)
- Cinnamon (1 tbsp.)
- Baking powder (.5 tbsp.)
- Coconut oil (2 tbsp.)
- Large egg (1)
- Sugar-free caramel syrup (.25 cup)
- Vanilla extract (1 tsp.)
- Pumpkin puree (.5 cup)

- Slivered almonds (.5 cup)
- Apple cider vinegar (1 tsp.)

Prep Technique:

1. Set the oven temperature to 350º Fahrenheit.
2. Use a deep mixing container to mix all of the fixings and stir well.
3. Place 6 paper liners in the muffin tin and add 1/4 cup of batter to each one.
4. Sprinkle several almonds on the tops, pressing gently. Bake for approximately 15 minutes or until the top is set.

Chocolate Chip Covered Muffins

Servings Provided: 15 (2 mini muffins per serving)
Cooking & Prep Time: 10 min.
Macro Counts For Each Serving:

- **Protein**: 1.6 g
- **Fat Content**: 3.8 g
- **Calories**: 45
- **Total Net Carbs**: 0.6 g

Ingredient List:

- Powdered erythritol (2 tbsp.)

- Fine almond flour (1 cup)
- Milk - your choice (.25 cup)
- Large egg or Flax egg (1)
- Baking powder (.5 tbsp.)
- Salt (25 tsp.)
- *Optional:* Mini chocolate chips/crushed walnuts/ pinch of cinnamon/etc.

Prep Technique:

1. Warm the oven to reach 350° Fahrenheit.
2. Grease a mini muffin tin.
3. Combine all of the dry fixings (stirring well). Then, stir in the wet. Scoop into muffin cups, filling about 2/3 of the way up the sides of the tins.
4. Bake for 10 minutes on the center rack.
5. Remove from the oven and let cool for 10 minutes (very important for firming).
6. Carefully go around the sides of each muffin with a knife and serve.

Chocolate Hazelnut Muffins

Servings Provided: 12

Cooking & Prep Time: 30 min.

Macro Counts For Each Serving:

- **Protein**: 8 g
- **Fat Content**: 25 g
- **Calories**: 282
- **Total Net Carbs**: 6 g

Ingredient List:

- Almond flour (3 cups)
- Coconut oil, melted (.5 cup)
- Large eggs (4 whisked)
- Nutmeg (.5 tsp.)
- Cloves (.25 tsp.)
- Chopped hazelnuts (.5 cup)
- Stevia (to your liking)
- Salt (dash)
- Baking soda (1 tsp.)
- 100% dark chocolate, broken into chunks (3 oz.)

Prep Technique:

1. Set the oven temperature to 350° Fahrenheit.
2. Mix the coconut oil, eggs, almond flour, nutmeg, cloves, sweetener, salt, baking soda, and chopped hazelnuts.
3. Pour the mixture into 12 lined or greased muffin pans.

4. Toss chocolate chunks into the top each muffin, pressing them down into the dough.
5. Bake for 18-20 minutes. Serve when ready or cool to store.

Chocolate Zucchini Muffins

Servings Provided: 12

Cooking & Prep Time: 35-40 min.

Macro Counts For Each Serving:

- **Protein**: 4 g
- **Fat Content**: 16 g
- **Calories**: 179
- **Total Net Carbs**: 3 g

Ingredient List:

- Eggs (5)
- Erythritol or your favorite low-carb sweetener (.75 cup)
- Coconut oil or Melted butter (.5 cup)
- Salt - see note (.5 tsp.)
- Cocoa powder - unsweetened (3 tbsp.)
- Vanilla extract (.75 cup)
- Shredded zucchini (1 cup)
- Almond flour (1 cup)

- Baking soda (.5 tsp.)
- Coconut flour (.5 cup)
- Baking powder (.5 tsp.)
- Cinnamon (.5 tsp.)
- *Also Needed:* Cooking oil spray
- 12-count muffin baking mold

Prep Technique:

1. Set the oven temperature at 325° Fahrenheit.
2. Lightly spritz the muffin molds with some cooking oil spray.
3. Mix the sweetener and butter or oil.
4. Whisk and add in the eggs; adding the vanilla, cocoa, and zucchini.
5. In another container, combine all of the fixings and add the batter to the prepared molds.
6. Bake for 25 to 30 minutes.
7. *Notes*: The net carbs listed are if you use erythritol.
8. Omit the salt if using salted butter.
9. Transfer the muffins from the molds to cool on a wire rack.

Coconut Flour Cranberry Pumpkin Muffins

Servings Provided: 12

Cooking & Prep Time: 45 min.

Macro Counts For Each Serving:

- **Protein**: 2.6 g
- **Fat Content**: 7.5 g
- **Calories**: 100
- **Total Net Carbs**: 3.8 g

Ingredient List:

- Coconut flour sifted (.5 cup)
- Baking powder (1.5 tsp.)
- Ground ginger (.25 tsp.)
- Cinnamon (.75 tsp.)
- Nutmeg (.25 tsp.)
- Ground cloves (.125 tsp.)
- Salt (.25 tsp.)
- Low-carb sweetener - ex. Swerve (.5 cup)
- Sukrin Gold packed or another brown sugar substitute (.25 cup)
- Pumpkin puree (1 cup)
- Soft/Melted butter (2 tbsp.)
- Heavy cream (.5 cup)
- Large eggs (3)

- Sugar-free dried cranberries (.66 cup)
- Cooking oil non-stick spray - as needed
- *Also Needed*: 12-count muffin tins with liners

Prep Technique:
1. Warm the oven to 375° Fahrenheit.
2. Prepare the muffin tins.
3. Sift or whisk the coconut flour with the baking powder, and spices.
4. Use the medium setting of an electric mixer to combine the rest of the fixings (sweeteners, cream, pumpkin, butter, and eggs).
5. Combine everything using the low speed just until combined.
6. Fold in cranberries. Scoop the batter into the cups.
7. Bake for 25-30 minutes. The centers are springy to the touch when they're ready.
8. Arrange the slightly cooled muffins on a wire rack to cool before storing.

Coconut Lemon Muffins

Servings Provided: 16

Cooking & Prep Time: 30 min.

Macro Counts For Each Serving:

- **Protein**: 3 g
- **Fat Content**: 7 g
- **Calories**: 78
- **Total Net Carbs**: 2 g

Ingredient List:

- Erythritol (.25 cup)
- Butter (.25 cup)
- Eggs (3)
- Coconut flour (.25 cup)
- Coconut flakes (.5 cup)
- Baking powder (.5 tsp.)
- Vanilla extract (.5 tsp.)
- Coconut milk (3 tbsp.)
- Lemon - juice & zest (1)

Prep Technique:

1. Warm the oven to 400° Fahrenheit.
2. Lightly grease 16 muffin tins. Whisk the butter and erythritol together until creamy.
3. Break the eggs in one at a time. Add the lemon juice, zest, milk, and vanilla extract. Stir in the baking powder, sifted flour, and flaked coconut.
4. Scoop the dough into the baking pan.

5. Prepare for 20 minutes in the heated oven. Cool slightly and enjoy. Cool thoroughly before storing.

Coffee Cake Muffins

Servings Provided: 12

Cooking & Prep Time: 60 min.

Macro Counts For Each Serving:

- **Protein**: 7 g
- **Fat Content**: 18 g
- **Calories**: 222
- **Total Net Carbs**: 5 g

Ingredient List - The Batter:

- Unchilled butter (2 tbsp.)
- Unchilled cream cheese (2 oz.)
- Stevia or favorite sweetener (.33 cup)
- Eggs (4)
- Vanilla (2 tsp.)
- Unsweetened vanilla almond milk (.5 cup)
- Almond flour (1 cup)
- Coconut flour (.5 cup)
- Baking powder (1 tsp.)
- Salt (.25 tsp.)

Ingredient List - The Topping:

- Almond flour (1 cup)
- Coconut flour (2 tbsp.)
- Stevia/your choice (.25 cup)
- Softened butter (.25 cup)
- Cinnamon (1 tsp.)
- *Optional*: Molasses (.5 tsp.)
- *Also Needed*: Standard muffin tin & Parchment baking paper

Prep Technique:

1. Soften the butter and cream cheese for about 30 minutes on the countertop before preparing the recipe.
2. Warm the oven to reach 350° Fahrenheit.
3. Prepare the tin with a spritz of cooking oil spray.
4. Combine all the batter fixings in a food processor. Mix thoroughly and pour into the muffin tin.
5. Combine the topping fixings in the food processor. Pulse until crumbs form. Sprinkle on top of the batter.
6. Bake 20-25 min until golden.
7. *Note:* If the crumb topping starts to get too dark cover with foil for the last 5 minutes.

Double-Chocolate Blender Muffins

Servings Provided: 9

Cooking & Prep Time: 45-50 min.

Macro Counts For Each Serving:

- **Protein**: 6.3 g
- **Fat Content**: 17.2 g
- **Calories**: 204
- **Total Net Carbs**: 4.8 g

Ingredient List:

- Large eggs (3)
- Almond milk/water (.5 cup)
- Almond flour (1 cup)
- Cocoa powder (.25 cup)
- Coconut flour (.25 cup)
- Swerve sweetener (.25 cup)
- Baking powder (2 tsp.)
- Salt (.25 tsp.)
- Avocado oil (or melted coconut oil (.25 cup)
- Vanilla extract (1 tsp.)
- Sugar-free chocolate chips (.33 cup)

Prep Technique:

1. Set the oven temperature to 325° Fahrenheit.

2. Line a 9-count muffin tin with a sheet of parchment baking paper.

3. Use a high-speed blender to mix the eggs, vanilla extract, and almond milk.

4. Pulse and toss in the dry fixings (cocoa powder, almond flour, swerve sweetener, coconut flour, baking powder, and salt).

5. Blend using the med-high setting until smooth, scraping the sides as needed. Add melted coconut oil and mix well until combined.

6. Stir in all but 1 tbsp. of chocolate chips.

7. Divide the batter evenly among the prepared muffin cups and top each with a few more chocolate chips.

8. Bake until firm to the touch (22 to 25 min.). Cool in the pan.

English Muffin

Servings Provided: 1

Cooking & Prep Time: Varies - depending on method

Macro Counts For Each Serving:

- **Protein**: 8 g
- **Fat Content**: 12 g
- **Calories**: 200

- **Total Net Carbs**: 2.5 g

Ingredient List:
- Melted butter or coconut oil (.5 tbsp.)
- Unsweetened almond/coconut milk/Half & Half (1 tbsp.)
- Whisked egg (1)
- Baking powder (.5 tsp.)
- Coconut flour (1 tbsp.)
- *Optional*: Vanilla extract (.125 tsp.)
- *Optional*: Liquid stevia (6 drops)
- *Optional*: Sea Salt (1 pinch)

Prep Technique:
1. Set the oven temperature to 400° Fahrenheit.
2. Melt the oil/butter in a ramekin. Add the remainder of the fixings to the bowl. Stir quickly until the clumps are gone.
3. Prepare in the microwave for 1.5 minutes or bake for 12 to 15 minutes.
4. Loosen the edges and transfer to a cutting surface. Slice in half sideways.
5. Lightly brown on each side in a skillet prepared with oil or butter. Gently press the muffins in the pan with the spatula as they toast.

6. Serve as desired.

French Toast Muffins

Servings Provided: 4

Cooking & Prep Time: 30 min.

Macro Counts For Each Serving:

- **Protein**: 6 g
- **Fat Content**: 33 g
- **Calories**: 316
- **Total Net Carbs**: 1 g

Ingredient List:

- Almond flour (.33 cup)
- Baking powder (.5 tsp.)
- Egg (1 whisked)
- Melted ghee (2.5 tbsp.)
- Stevia (dash)

Ingredient List - French Toast Mixture:

- Coconut cream (.25 cup)
- Melted ghee (.25 cup)
- Eggs (2 whisked)
- Erythritol (.25 cup)
- Vanilla extract (1 tbsp.)

- Ground cinnamon (1 tbsp.)

Prep Technique:

1. Set the oven temperature at 350° Fahrenheit.
2. Mix the bread fixings together in a microwaveable bowl and microwave for

    two minutes using the high heat temperature setting.
3. Let cool and chop into cubes.
4. Grease muffin cups with ghee. Divide the chopped cubes of bread between

    the four muffin cups.
5. Mix together the French toast mixture. Pour into four muffin cups

    and let soak for 20 minutes.
6. Bake for 20 minutes and serve.

Gingerbread Blender Muffins

Servings Provided: 12

Cooking & Prep Time: 40-45 min.

Macro Counts For Each Serving:

- **Protein**: 8.3 g
- **Fat Content**: 17.1 g
- **Calories**: 205

- **Total Net Carbs**: 3.7 g

Ingredient List:
- Sour cream (.5 cup)
- Eggs (4 large)
- Vanilla extract (1 tsp.)
- Almond flour (3 cups)
- Sweetener equivalent to .75 cup sugar
- Cocoa powder (1 tbsp.)
- Baking powder (2 tsp.)
- Cinnamon (1 tsp.)
- Cloves (.25 tsp.)
- Ginger (2 tsp.)
- Salt (.25 tsp.)

Prep Technique:
1. Warm the oven to reach 325° Fahrenheit before baking time.
2. Prepare a muffin tin with parchment baking paper or silicone liners.
3. Combine the sour cream, eggs, and vanilla in a large blender jar. Blend for about 30 seconds.
4. Sift and add the almond flour, sweetener, cocoa powder, baking powder, spices, and salt. Blend again until well combined.

5. Divide the mixture among the prepared muffin cups.

6. Bake until golden brown and firm to the touch (25-30 min.).

Lemon Poppyseed Muffins

Servings Provided: 12

Cooking & Prep Time: 55 min.

Macro Counts For Each Serving:

- **Protein**: 4 g
- **Fat Content**: 13 g
- **Calories**: 141
- **Total Net Carbs**: 1 g

Ingredient List:

- Eggs (3)
- Full-fat ricotta cheese (.25 cup)
- Coconut oil (.25 cup)
- Poppy seeds (2 tbsp.)
- True lemon packets (4)
- Heavy whipping cream (.25 cup)
- Lemon extract (1 tsp.)
- Almond flour (1 cup)
- Swerve or alternative sweetener (.33 cup)

- Baking powder (1 tsp.)

Prep Technique:

1. Warm the oven to reach 350⁰ Fahrenheit
2. Prepare a 12-count muffin tin with silicone cupcake liners.
3. Combine all of the fixings until smooth and scrape into the cups.
4. Bake for 40 minutes.
5. Chill for several minutes before taking them from the liners.

Pancake & Berry Muffins

Servings Provided: 8

Cooking & Prep Time: 30-35 min.

Macro Counts For Each Serving:

- **Protein**: 8.3 g
- **Fat Content**: 17.1 g
- **Calories**: 211
- **Total Net Carbs**: 4.6 g

Ingredient List:

- Plain whole milk yogurt (.5 cup)
- Melted coconut oil (2 tbsp.)

- Swerve sweetener or equivalent of choice (3 tbsp.)
- Apple cider vinegar (.25 tsp.)
- Vanilla extract (1 tsp.)
- Blanched almond flour (1.75 cups)
- Salt (.25 cup)
- Baking soda (.5 tsp.)
- Large eggs (3)
- Frozen blueberries and raspberries (.5 cup)
- *Also Needed*: 8-count muffin cups with parchment liners or spritz the cups with cooking oil spray

Prep Technique:

1. Warm the oven to reach 350° Fahrenheit.
2. Prepare the muffin tin.
3. Use a blender to combine the yogurt, sweetener, butter, vanilla, and vinegar. Add the salt, almond flour, and baking soda. Blend on low for about 15 seconds until well incorporated.
4. Toss in the eggs to pulse for 15 to 20 seconds. Then, blend on high for another 20 to 30 seconds until the batter is combined.
5. Add all but two tablespoons of the frozen berries to the batter.
6. Stir in by hand - *Don't Blend!*

7. Pour the prepared batter in the muffin cups. Garnish with berries on top.
8. Bake until slightly golden brown (15 to 18 min.).
9. Transfer to the countertop to cool in its pan for about five minutes. Serve.

Pumpkin Cream Cheese Muffins

Servings Provided: 12

Cooking & Prep Time: 60-70 min.

Macro Counts For Each Serving:
- **Protein**: 7.5 g
- **Fat Content**: 18.4 g
- **Calories**: 221
- **Total Net Carbs**: 3.8 g

Ingredient List -Muffins:
- Almond flour (2 cups)
- Swerve sweetener (.5 cup)
- Baking powder (2 tsp.)
- Unflavored whey protein powder (.25 cup)
- Pumpkin pie spice (2 tsp.)
- Salt (.5 tsp.)
- Large eggs (2)
- Pumpkin puree (.5 cup)

- Butter - melted (.25 cup)
- Unsweetened almond milk (.25 cup)
- Vanilla extract (.5 tsp.)

Ingredient List - Filling:

- Powdered Swerve sweetener (3 tbsp.)
- Cream cheese softened (6 oz.)
- Heavy cream (1 tbsp.)
- Vanilla (.5 tsp.)

Prep Technique:

1. Warm the oven to reach 325° Fahrenheit.
2. Prepare the filling by mixing all of the components.
3. Prepare a muffin tin with parchment or silicone liners.
4. Whisk the almond flour, protein powder, pumpkin pie spice, sweetener, salt, and baking powder.
5. Break the eggs into the mixture. Mix in the melted butter, almond milk, pumpkin puree, and vanilla extract. Mix until well combined.
6. Drop a spoonful of batter into the pans. Make a well in the center.

7. Drop a tablespoon of cream cheese filling into the well, and top with more batter to cover the cream cheese mixture.

8. Bake for about 25 minutes. Cool in pan 15 minutes before transferring to a wire rack to cool completely.

9. *Note:* Make your own pumpkin spice using 1 tsp. cinnamon, .5 tsp. ginger, and .25 tsp. . . . . cloves.

Pumpkin Maple Flaxseed Muffins

Servings Provided: 10

Cooking & Prep Time: 25-30 min.

Macro Counts For Each Serving:

- **Protein**: 5 g
- **Fat Content**: 8.5 g
- **Calories**: 120
- **Total Net Carbs**: 2 g

Ingredient List:

- Ground flaxseeds (1.25 cups)
- Baking powder (.5 tbsp.)
- Erythritol (.33 cup)
- Cinnamon (1 tbsp.)

- Salt (.5 tsp.)
- Pumpkin pie spice (1 tbsp.)
- Egg (1)
- Coconut oil (2 tbsp.)
- Pure pumpkin puree (1 cup)
- Apple cider vinegar (.5 tsp.)
- Maple syrup (.5 cup)
- Vanilla extract (.5 tsp.)
- *Topping*: Pumpkin seeds

Prep Technique:

1. Heat the oven to 350° Fahrenheit.
2. Prepare the muffin tin with cupcake liners.
3. Toss the seeds into the blender about one second – no longer or it could become damp.
4. Combine the dry fixings and whisk until well mixed. Add the puree, vanilla extract, and pumpkin spice along with the maple syrup (.5 tsp.) if using.
5. Blend in the oil, egg, and apple cider vinegar. Combine nuts or any other fold-ins of your choice, but also add the carbs.
6. Scoop the mixture out by the tablespoon in the prepared tins. Garnish with some of the pumpkin

seeds. Leave a little space in the top since they will rise.

7. Bake for approximately 20 minutes. They are ready when they are slightly browned. Let them cool a few minutes and add some ghee or butter or some more syrup.

Pumpkin Spice Mug Muffin

Servings Provided: 1

Cooking & Prep Time: 4-5 min.

Macro Counts For Each Serving:

- **Protein**: 11 g
- **Fat Content**: 44 g
- **Calories**: 456
- **Total Net Carbs**: 3 g

Ingredient List:

- Egg (1)
- Almond flour (.25 cup)
- Baking powder (.25 tsp.)
- Ghee (2 tbsp.)
- Cinnamon powder (1 tbsp.)
- Ground nutmeg (1 dash)
- Ground ginger (1 dash)

- Allspice (1 dash)
- Vanilla extract (1 tsp.)
- Erythritol (1 tbsp.)
- Stevia (1 dash)

Prep Technique:

1. Whisk each of the fixings in a mug suitable for the microwave.
2. Prepare for 90 seconds using the high-temperature setting.
3. Eat it right out of the mug or tip it onto a serving dish.

Strawberry Glazed Muffins

Servings Provided: 12

Cooking & Prep Time: 40 min.

Macro Counts For Each Serving:

- **Protein**: 7 g
- **Fat Content**: 25 g
- **Calories**: 257
- **Total Net Carbs**: 3 g

Ingredient List:

- Almond flour (3 cups)

- Ghee (.5 cup - melted
- Large eggs (3 whisked)
- Lemon zest (1 tbsp.)
- Vanilla extract (1 tbsp.)
- Erythritol (.25 cup)
- Baking soda (1 tsp.)
- Fresh strawberries (1 cup chopped)

Ingredient List - The Glaze:

- Coconut cream (4 tbsp.)
- Erythritol (1 tbsp.)

Prep Technique:

1. Preheat oven to 350° Fahrenheit.
2. Mix together all the muffin fixings in a large mixing bowl.
3. Add the chopped strawberries and fold in gently.
4. Pour into muffin pans (use silicone muffin pans or grease the metal pans).
5. Bake for 16-18 minutes. Let cool completely.
6. Make the glaze. Mix all the glaze fixings together and cool to room temperature so it thickens - but isn't solid. Drizzle or spread over the cooled muffins.

Other Options

Cauliflower Bacon & Cheese Muffins

Servings Provided: 6 - 2 each

Cooking & Prep Time: 45 min.

Macro Counts For Each Serving:

- **Protein**: 6.6 g
- **Fat Content**: 8 g
- **Calories**: 110
- **Total Net Carbs**: 2.4 g

Ingredient List:

- Chopped bacon (7 slices)
- Cauliflower rice (3 cups)
- Baking powder (1 tsp.)
- Almond flour (.25 cup)
- Oregano (1 tbsp.)
- Garlic powder (1 tbsp.)
- Parsley (1 tbsp.)
- Salt and pepper (to taste)
- Paprika (1 tbsp.)
- Shredded cheddar cheese (1 cup)
- Large eggs (2)
- Crumbled feta (.25 cup)

Prep Technique:

1. Set the oven temperature to 350º Fahrenheit.
2. Prepare the riced cauliflower. Cook, drain, and chop the bacon.
3. Fold in each of the dry fixings with the bacon and cheese. Whisk and add the eggs and mix well.
4. Prepare a 12-count muffin tin with baking cups. Add the mixture to each one and top off with the feta cheese.
5. Bake for 35 minutes and serve.

Coconut Bacon Egg Muffins

Servings Provided: 12

Cooking & Prep Time: 40 min.

Macro Counts For Each Serving:

- **Protein**: 7 g
- **Fat Content**: 20 g
- **Calories**: 224
- **Total Net Carbs**: 1 g

Ingredient List:

- Medium eggs (6)
- Coconut flour (.75 cup)
- Coconut oil (.25 cup)

- Bacon (12 slices)
- Chives (.25 cup)

Prep Technique:

1. Warm the oven to reach 350° Fahrenheit.
2. Prepare the bacon and chop to bits. Finely chop the chives.
3. Combine all of the fixings and pour into the muffin cups.
4. Bake until they are solid or about 25-30 minutes.
5. Cool slightly and serve.

Cornbread Muffins

Servings Provided: 6
Cooking & Prep Time: 30 min.
Macro Counts For Each Serving:

- **Protein**: 6 g
- **Fat Content**: 17 g
- **Calories**: 191
- **Total Net Carbs**: 2 g

Ingredient List:

- Almond flour (.75 cup)
- Coconut flour (.25 cup)

- Baking powder (2 tsp.)
- Salt (1 tsp.)
- Ghee (2 tbsp.)
- Eggs (3)
- Coconut milk (.5 cup)

Prep Technique:

1. Warm the oven to 350° Fahrenheit.
2. Grease a muffin pan with coconut oil/muffin liners or a silicone muffin pan.
3. Combine all of the fixings and mix well in a large bowl.
4. Pour the batter into the muffin pan.
5. Bake for about 20 minutes.

Green Eggs & Ham Muffins

Servings Provided: 12

Cooking & Prep Time: 40 min.

Macro Counts For Each Serving:

- **Protein**: 29 g
- **Fat Content**: 18 g
- **Calories**: 295
- **Total Net Carbs**: 3 g

Ingredient List:

- Broccoli (1 cup)
- Eggs (10 whisked)
- Ham (10 slices - diced)
- Onion (.5 of 1)
- Coconut milk from the can (.5 cup)
- Salt and pepper (as desired)
- Baking powder (1 tsp.)

Prep Technique:

1. Set the oven to 350° Fahrenheit.
2. Finely chop the broccoli and onion. Dice the ham.
3. Combine everything together in a large mixing bowl.
4. Dump the batter into greased muffin cups.
5. Bake for 25-30 minutes or until the middle of the muffins is solid.

Jalapeno Muffins

Servings Provided: 12

Cooking & Prep Time: 30 min.

Macro Counts For Each Serving:

- **Protein**: 3 g
- **Fat Content**: 8 g

- **Calories**: 96
- **Total Net Carbs**: 0 g

Ingredient List:
- Almond flour (.75 cup)
- Coconut flour (.25 cup)
- Baking powder (2 tsp.)
- Salt (1 dash)
- Stevia or erythritol (as desired)
- Ghee or coconut oil, melted but not hot (2 tbsp.)
- Eggs (3 whisked)
- Coconut milk (.75 cup)
- Jalapeno chili peppers (4 deseeded and finely diced)

Prep Technique:
1. Set the oven to 350° Fahrenheit.
2. Place all the dry fixings into a large mixing bowl and mix well.
3. Add in the ghee/coconut oil, whisked eggs, and coconut milk.
4. Fold in the chopped jalapeno pepper pieces.
5. Pour the mixture into a greased muffin tray or use muffin liners.

6. Bake until a toothpick inserted into the middle of a muffin comes out clean (18-20 min.).

Onion & Squash Muffins

Servings Provided: 6

Cooking & Prep Time: 35 min.

Macro Counts For Each Serving:

- **Protein**: 7 g
- **Fat Content**: 8 g
- **Calories**: 222
- **Total Net Carbs**: 3 g

Ingredient List:

- Salt (as desired)
- Baking powder (.66 tsp.)
- Almond flour (1 cup)
- Peeled & grated squash (1)
- Chopped spring onions (2-3 sprigs)
- Olive oil (1 tbsp.)
- Egg (1)
- Plain yogurt (.25 cup)
- Grated hard cheese (.5 cup)

Prep Technique:

1. Warm up the oven to 350° Fahrenheit.

2. Spritz six muffin tins with cooking oil spray.

3. Season the grated squash with salt and set aside.

4. Combine the baking powder, salt, and sifted flour.

5. Whisk the egg and mix with the oil, about half of the cheese, and yogurt. Combine well.

6. Fold in the squash and juices into the dough. Work in the chopped onions and add to the prepared muffin cups (1/2 full). Sprinkle with the cheese, and bake for 25 minutes.

7. Cool slightly and serve.

Chapter 7: Keto Cookies

Almond Nut Butter Cookies

Servings Provided: 10

Cooking & Prep Time: 28-30 min.

Macro Counts For Each Serving:

- **Protein**: 5 g
- **Fat Content**: 22 g
- **Calories**: 235
- **Total Net Carbs**: 7 g

Ingredient List:

- Almond butter (8.8 oz.)
- Egg (1)
- Salted butter (.25 tsp.)

- Raw coconut butter (.25 cup)
- Powdered erythritol (.25 cup)

Prep Technique:

1. Set the oven temperature to 320º Fahrenheit. Prepare a cookie sheet with a sheet of parchment paper.
2. Use a double boiler to melt the almond butter. Take it from the burner and stir in the salt, erythritol, and egg until well mixed.
3. Break into ten pieces and roll into balls.
4. Arrange on a prepared pan and flatten with a fork or your hand.
5. Bake for 12 minutes or until browned.

Almond Shortbread Cookies

Servings Provided: 24

Cooking & Prep Time: 1 hr. 35 min.

Macro Counts For Each Serving:

- **Protein**: 1 g
- **Fat Content**: 5 g
- **Calories**: 59
- **Total Net Carbs**: 1 g

Ingredient List:

- Almond flour (1.5 cups)
- Xanthan gum (.5 tsp.)
- Kosher salt (.25 tsp.)
- Unchilled grass-fed butter (6 tbsp.)
- Powdered erythritol (6 tbsp.)
- Vanilla extract (.5 tsp.)
- *Optional: For the Coating*: Melted dark chocolate & Flaky sea salt

Prep Technique:

1. Sift the almond flour into a dry skillet. Toast using medium heat until golden (3-6 min.). Transfer from the pan, whisk in the salt, and xanthan gum. Set aside for now to cool.
2. Cream the butter in a mixing container using an electric mixer (2-3 min.).
3. Toss in the sweetener and vanilla extract.
4. With your mixer on low, add half of the almond flour mixture, stirring until just combined and add in with the remainder of the mixture.
5. Wrap the dough in a cling-type film and store in the fridge for at least an hour.
6. Warm the oven to 350° Fahrenheit.

7. Roll out the dough between parchment paper layers and either simply slice with a knife. Arrange the shaped cookies on a cookie sheet. Place in the freezer for about 15 minutes to firm before baking.

8. Bake using these times, (15-18 minutes for the larger ones) or (10-13 minutes for the small ones).

9. Cool the pan because they will crumble when warm.

Chocolate Macaroon Cookies With Coconut

Servings Provided: 20

Cooking & Prep Time: 30 min.

Macro Counts For Each Serving:

- **Protein**: 2.2 g
- **Fat Content**: 7 g
- **Calories**: 77
- **Total Net Carbs**: 1 g

Ingredient List:

- Almond flour (1 cup)
- Coconut flour (3 tbsp.)
- Cocoa powder (.25 cup)

- Baking powder (.5 tsp.)
- Erythritol (.33 cup)
- Shredded unsweetened coconut (.33 cup)
- Salt (.25 tsp.)
- Unchilled eggs (2)
- Coconut oil (.25 cup)
- Vanilla extract (1 tsp.)

Prep Technique:

1. Line a baking tin with a layer of aluminum foil.
2. Warm the oven to reach 350º Fahrenheit.
3. Sift all of the dry fixings into a mixing container. Slowly add the wet components, mixing well.
4. Roll the dough into small balls and place on the prepared pan – several inches apart.
5. Bake for 15 to 20 minutes.
6. Sprinkle using the shredded coconut, and serve.

Chocolate & Orange Cookies

Servings Provided: 16

Cooking & Prep Time: 35 min.

Macro Counts For Each Serving:

- **Protein**: 17 g
- **Fat Content**: 14 g

- **Calories**: 155
- **Total Net Carbs**: 10 g

Ingredient List:

- Butter (7 tbsp.)
- Almond flour (2 cups)
- Granulated sweetener (.75 cup)
- Dark chocolate (2 oz.)
- Eggs (2)
- Orange zest (1 tbsp.)
- Orange extract (1 tsp.)
- Vanilla extract (1 tsp.)
- Orange juice (1 tbsp.)
- Baking powder (.75 tsp.)
- Baking soda (.5 tsp.)
- Salt (.5 tsp.)

Prep Technique:

1. Set the oven temperature at 350º Fahrenheit.
2. Combine the dry fixings (flour, baking powder, baking soda, salt, and sweetener).
3. Use a microwavable dish to melt the butter and stir in the orange zest, juice, orange extract, and vanilla extract.
4. Combine all of the fixings, mixing well.

5. Add the dough onto a baking tin. Form into a rectangle and slice into 16 servings.
6. Bake for 20-25 minutes.

Chocolate Sea Salt Cookies

Servings Provided: 15

Cooking & Prep Time: 50-55 min.

Macro Counts For Each Serving:
- **Protein**: 3.4 g
- **Fat Content**: 18.2 g
- **Calories**: 188
- **Total Net Carbs**: 1.6 g

Ingredient List:
- Unchilled coconut oil (.75 cup)
- Eggs (2)
- Vanilla extract (1 tsp.)
- Golden monk fruit sweetener (.75 cup)
- Unsweetened cocoa powder (2 tbsp.)
- Salt (.5 tsp.)
- Cream of tartar (.25 tsp.)
- Baking soda (.5 tsp.)
- Almond flour (2 cups)
- Flaky sea salt (to your liking)

Prep Technique:

1. Heat the oven to reach 350º Fahrenheit.
2. Set up two baking sheets with a layer of parchment baking paper.
3. Prepare using a hand mixer. Combine the eggs, coconut oil, and vanilla extract.
4. Toss in the sweetener, baking soda, cocoa powder, salt, and cream of tartar. Mix thoroughly.
5. Gradually fold in the almond flour.
6. Form the dough into balls. Place onto the baking sheet. Arrange them about two to three inches apart.
7. Garnish using the sea salt on top of each cookie.
8. Bake cookies for about 16 to 20 minutes; baking one tray at a time.
9. Remove and cool completely.
10. Gently pull the paper away from each of the cookies. Serve.

Chocolate Zucchini Cookies

Servings Provided: 12

Cooking & Prep Time: 25-30 min.

Macro Counts For Each Serving:

- **Protein**: 3 g
- **Fat Content**: 13 g
- **Calories**: 140
- **Total Net Carbs**: 2 g

Ingredient List:
- Grated zucchini (1 cup)
- Almond flour (1 cup)
- Baking soda (.5 tsp.)
- Coconut flour (.25 cup)
- Cacao powder or unsweetened cocoa powder (.25 cup)
- Salt (.5 tsp.)
- Cinnamon (.25 tsp.)
- Monk fruit sweetener or raw honey (.5 cup)
- Butter flavored coconut oil or ghee (.33 cup)
- Vanilla extract (1 tsp.)
- Large egg yolk (1)
- *Optional*: Sugar-free chocolate chips or dark chocolate pieces (.25 cup)

Prep Technique:
1. Prepare the zucchini, and wrap it in a towel to squeeze out excess liquid.

2. Whisk the dry fixings (salt, almond flour, cacao powder, coconut flour, cinnamon, and baking soda). Put it to the side for now.
3. In a glass mixing bowl, melt the coconut oil/ghee.
4. Whisk in the sweetener, egg yolk, and vanilla extract.
5. Stir the zucchini into the sweetened mixture and combine with the dry ingredients. Fold in chocolate if using.
6. Shape the dough tbsp.-sized balls by rolling in your hands.
7. Flatten each ball out and top each with a few pieces of chocolate.
8. Bake at 350° Fahrenheit for 10 to 12 minutes.

Cinnamon Cookies

Servings Provided: 8

Cooking & Prep Time: 27-30 min.

Macro Counts For Each Serving:

- **Protein**: 5 g
- **Fat Content**: 25 g
- **Calories**: 260
- **Total Net Carbs**: 6 g

Ingredient List:

- Almond meal (2 cups)
- Salted butter (.5 cup)
- Stevia (.5 cup)
- Cinnamon (1 tsp.)
- Vanilla (1 tsp.)

Prep Technique:

1. Warm the oven to reach 300° Fahrenheit.
2. Combine each of the fixings and shape into balls.
3. Prepare a cookie tin with a layer of parchment paper.
4. Arrange the cookies in the pan and press with a fork to flatten.
5. Bake for 20 to 25 minutes. Check when approaching the 18-minute marker.

Coconut No-Bake Cookies

Servings Provided: 20

Cooking & Prep Time: 60 min.

Macro Counts For Each Serving:

- **Protein**: 3 g
- **Fat Content**: 10 g
- **Calories**: 99

- **Total Net Carbs**: 0 g

Ingredient List:

- Melted coconut oil (1 cup)
- Monk fruit sweetened maple syrup or your favorite (.5 cup)
- Shredded unsweetened coconut flakes (3 cups)

Prep Technique:

1. Cut out a sheet of parchment paper and place on a cookie tray.
2. Combine all of the fixings.
3. Run your hands through some water from the tap and shape the mixture into small balls. Arrange them in the pan around one to two inches apart.
4. Press them down to form a cookie and refrigerate until firm.
5. You can prepare these into individual bags if you're an on-the-go kind of person. It will stay fresh covered for up to 7 days (room temperature). Store in the fridge for up to a month or frozen up to two months.

Coconut & Chocolate Cookies

Servings Provided: 20

Cooking & Prep Time: 25 min.

Macro Counts For Each Serving:

- **Protein**: 2.2 g
- **Fat Content**: 6.8 g
- **Calories**: 77
- **Total Net Carbs**: 1 g

Ingredient List:

- Almond flour (1 cup)
- Unsweetened shredded coconut (.33 cup)
- Erythritol (.33 cup)
- Baking powder (.5 tsp.)
- Cocoa powder (.25 cup)
- Coconut oil (.25 cup)
- Coconut flour (3 tbsp.)
- Salt (.25 tsp.)
- Vanilla extract (.25 tsp.)
- Un-chilled eggs (2)

Prep Technique:

1. Warm the oven to 350° Fahrenheit.
2. Cover a baking tin with a layer of parchment

paper.

3. Mix the dry fixings using a hand mi

4. In another bowl, combine the wet
   add to the dry until well blended.

5. Break apart pieces of the cookie dough and roll
   into 20 balls.

6. Arrange on the prepared pan.

7. Bake for 15 to 20 minutes.

Dark Chocolate Chip Cookies

Servings Provided: 18

Cooking & Prep Time: 25-30 min.

Macro Counts For Each Serving:

- **Protein**: 2 g
- **Fat Content**: 9 g
- **Calories**: 96
- **Total Net Carbs**: 1 g

Ingredient List:

- Eggs (2 large)
- Grass-fed melted butter (1 stick - .5 cup)
- Heavy cream (2 tbsp.)
- Pure vanilla extract - alcohol-free (2 tsp.)
- Almond flour (2.75 cups)

...her salt (.25 tsp.)

- Swerve (.5 cup or to taste)
- Dark chocolate chips - ex. Lily's (.75 cup)
- Cooking spray - as needed

Prep Technique:

1. Warm up the oven to 350° Fahrenheit. Prepare the pan.
2. Whisk the egg with the heavy cream, butter, vanilla, almond flour, salt, and swerve. Fold in the chocolate chips.
3. Form the mixture into one-inch balls.
4. Arrange the cookies about three inches apart onto the cookie sheets.
5. Bake until browned to your liking (17-19 min.).

Italian Almond Macaroons

Servings Provided: 45

Cooking & Prep Time: 1 hr. 15 min.

Macro Counts For Each Serving:

- **Protein**: 2 g
- **Fat Content**: 3 g
- **Calories**: 31
- **Total Net Carbs**: 0 g

Ingredient List:

- Almond flour about (2 cups plus 2 tbsp.)
- Monk fruit low-carb sweetener (.25 cup)
- Egg (2 whites)
- Almond extract (.5 tsp.)
- Powdered monk fruit sweetener - confectioners (1 tbsp.)

Prep Technique:

1. Prepare a cookie sheet with a layer of parchment baking paper.
2. Combine the almond flour, sweetener, egg whites, and almond extract.
3. Knead the mixture until the dough is formed.
4. Form the dough into one-inch balls and place on the pan at least 1 inch apart.
5. Bake at 250° Fahrenheit on the bottom rack of the oven for 55 to 60 minutes.
6. Remove the cookies from the baking pan to wire rack and dust using the confectioner's sweetener while still warm.

Italian Amaretti Cookies

Servings Provided: 16

Cooking & Prep Time: 25 min.

Macro Counts For Each Serving:

- **Protein**: 2.5 g
- **Fat Content**: 8 g
- **Calories**: 86
- **Total Net Carbs**: 1 g

Ingredient List:

- Coconut flour (2 tbsp.)
- Cinnamon (.25 tsp.)
- Baking powder (.5 tsp.)
- Erythritol (.5 cup)
- Salt (.5 tsp.)
- Almond flour (1 cup)
- Eggs (2)
- Almond extract (.5 tsp.)
- Vanilla extract (.5 tsp.)
- Coconut oil (4 tbsp.)
- Sugar-free jam (2 tbsp.)
- Shredded coconut (1 tbsp.)

Prep Technique:

1. Cover a baking tin with a sheet of parchment paper. Warm the oven to reach 400º Fahrenheit.

2. Sift the flour and combine all of the dry fixings. After combined, work in the wet ones. Shape into 16 cookies. Make a dent in the center of each one. Bake for 15 to 17 minutes.

3. Let them cool a few minutes before adding a dab of jam to each one and a sprinkle of coconut bits.

Low-Carb Chocolate Chip Cookies

Servings Provided: 24

Cooking & Prep Time: 55 min.

Macro Counts For Each Serving:

- **Protein**: 2 g
- **Fat Content**:8 g
- **Calories**: 90
- **Total Net Carbs**: 2 g

Ingredient List:

- Large egg (1)
- Swerve sweetener (.66 cup)
- Room temperature butter (5.5 tbsp.)
- Vanilla extract (.5 tsp.)
- Almond flour (1.25 cups)
- Sea salt - optional (.125 tsp.)
- Baking powder (1.5 tsp.)
- Coconut flour (1 tbsp.)
- Sugar-free chocolate chips (.5 cup)
- *Optional:* Molasses (.5 tsp.)
- *Optional:* Chopped pecans (.25 cup)

Prep Technique:

1. Use some parchment paper or silicone baking mats to line two baking sheets. Set the oven temperature to 325º Fahrenheit.
2. Use a mixer to blend the sweetener, butter, molasses, egg, and vanilla extract until well combined.
3. In another container, combine the two flours, sea salt, and baking powder. Stir until blended. Fold the pecans and chocolate chips into the mix.
4. Arrange the cookie dough by the tablespoonful into the pans. (They should be 1.5-inches apart.)
5. Bake until the bottoms are browned or about 12-15 minutes. Let them cool until firm and set (minimum 25 minutes).

Orange Cream Cheese Cookies & Nuts

Servings Provided: 18

Cooking & Prep Time: 35 min.

Macro Counts For Each Serving:

- **Protein**: 3 g
- **Fat Content**: 19 g
- **Calories**: 200
- **Total Net Carbs**: 2 g

Ingredient List:

- Softened butter (.75 cup)
- Eggs (3)
- Coconut flour (.5 cup)
- Baking powder (1.5 tsp.)
- Monk fruit sweetener (.75 cup)
- Baking soda (.25 tsp.)
- Sugar-free dried cranberries (.25 cup)
- Macadamia nuts chopped (.5 cup)
- Dried grated orange zest (1.5 tsp.)

Prep Technique:

1. In a mixing container, beat the sweetener with the eggs and butter until well combined.
2. Whisk or sift the coconut flour, baking powder, and soda. Beat on the low setting or with a spoon until fully mixed.
3. Fold in the berries, orange zest, and nuts.
4. Shape into rounds and arrange on the cookie sheet.
5. Arrange the cookies a minimum of one inch apart for baking on a parchment-lined cookie sheet. Press each mound down slightly to flatten.

6. Bake at 350° Fahrenheit until edges have started to brown or for eight to ten minutes. Cool on a cooling rack.

7. Enjoy right out of the fridge for a week or they can be frozen for longer storage.

Peanut Butter Cookies

Servings Provided: 27

Cooking & Prep Time: 25 min.

Macro Counts For Each Serving:

- **Protein**: 4 g
- **Fat Content**: 7 g
- **Calories**: 94
- **Total Net Carbs**: 2 g

Ingredient List:

- Peanut butter (creamy, salted (1.25 cups)
- Large eggs (2)
- Erythritol (or any granulated sweetener (.5 cup)
- Vanilla extract - optional (1 tsp.)
- Sea salt (.25 tsp.)
- Peanuts - coarsely chopped (.75 cup)

Prep Technique:

1. Coarsely chop the peanuts.
2. Warm up the oven to 350º Fahrenheit.
3. Prepare the pan with baking paper.
4. Place the egg, peanut butter, sweetener, salt, and vanilla into the food processor.
5. Process until smooth, scraping the sides if needed.
6. Pulse in the peanut pieces until just combined, leaving some pieces for crunch.
7. Tightly pack the dough into a scoop before releasing onto the sheet.
8. Flatten the cookies using a fork in a crisscross pattern. Bake for about 15 to 20 minutes.
9. Cool completely before handling.
10. *Notes:* Use .33 cup of sweetener for less sweet cookies. If you like salty-sweet use .5 tsp. of sea salt. Measure the peanuts whole and shelled.
11. The cookies will crisp as they cool.

Peanut Butter & Jelly Cookies

Servings Provided: 6

Cooking & Prep Time: 20 min.

Macro Counts For Each Serving:

- **Protein**: 9 g
- **Fat Content**: 18 g
- **Calories**: 209
- **Total Net Carbs**: 5 g

Ingredient List:

- Egg (1)
- Stevia sugar substitute (.5 cup)
- Creamy Keto-friendly peanut butter (.66 cup)
- Sugar-free strawberry preserves (.33 cup)
- Almond flour (.33 cup)
- Sea salt (.25 tsp.)
- Baking powder (.25 tsp.)
- Pure vanilla extract (.25 tsp.)

Prep Technique:

1. Warm up the oven to 350º Fahrenheit. Spray a cookie sheet with a spritz of cooking oil or prepare with a layer of parchment paper.
2. Whisk the egg, stevia, and peanut butter. When it's creamy, add the salt, baking powder, flour, and vanilla.
3. Mix well and shape into small balls. Make an indention in each one and add one teaspoon of preserves.
4. Bake until browned or for about 10 to 12 minutes.
5. Cool on a wire rack and serve.

Pistachio Cookies

Servings Provided: 16

Cooking & Prep Time: 45 min.

Macro Counts For Each Serving:

- **Protein**: 4 g
- **Fat Content**: 12 g
- **Calories**: 135
- **Total Net Carbs**: 2 g

Ingredient List:

- Melted butter (6 tbsp.)

- Chopped pistachios (.5 cup)
- Erythritol (.5 cup)
- Almond flour (2 cups)

Prep Technique:

1. Combine all of the ingredients together in a mixing container.
2. Shape the dough into a long roll and cover with a sheet of plastic wrap.
3. Place in the fridge for about 30 minutes. Unwrap and slice into 16 portions.
4. Bake for 12 to 15 minutes.

Pumpkin Cheesecake Cookies

Servings Provided: 15 cookies

Cooking & Prep Time: 25 min.

Macro Counts For Each Serving:

- **Protein**: 5 g
- **Fat Content**: 15 g
- **Calories**: 159
- **Total Net Carbs**: 2 g

Ingredient List:

- Softened butter (6 tbsp.)

- Almond flour (2 cups)
- Solid-pack pumpkin puree (.33 cup)
- Large egg (1)
- Granulated erythritol sweetener (.75 cup)
- Baking powder (.5 tsp.)
- Ground cinnamon (1 tsp.)
- Ground nutmeg (.25 tsp.)
- Ground allspice (.125 tsp.)
- Salt (1 pinch)

Ingredient List - The Filling:
- Cream cheese (4 oz.)
- Vanilla (.5 tsp.)
- Large egg (1)
- Granulated erythritol sweetener (2 tbsp.)

Prep Technique:
1. Warm the oven to reach 350° Fahrenheit.
2. Combine all of cookie dough fixings in a mixing bowl and mix well until a dough forms.
3. Scoop or spoon the cookie batter by about 1.5 tablespoons onto a parchment-lined baking sheet.
4. Use the back of the scoop or a round tablespoon measuring spoon to dent the tops of each cookie as shown in the photo collage in the post.

5. Combine the cream cheese, sweetener, egg, and vanilla in a magic bullet or small blender cup.

6. Blend until smooth.

7. Pour the cream cheese filling into the tops of each cookie dent.

8. Bake the cookies for 20 minutes, or until golden brown and the tops no longer jiggle.

9. Remove and cool at least 10 minutes before eating.

Snickerdoodles

Servings Provided: 16

Cooking & Prep Time: 25 min.

Macro Counts For Each Serving:

- **Protein**: 3 g
- **Fat Content**: 13 g
- **Calories**: 131
- **Total Net Carbs**: 1.5 g

Ingredient List - The Cookies:

- Superfine almond flour (2 cups)
- Softened salted butter (.5 cup)
- Kosher salt (1 pinch)
- Erythritol granulated sweetener (.75 cup)

- Baking soda (.5 tsp.)

Ingredient List - The Coating:
- Erythritol granulated sweetener (2 tbsp.)
- Ground cinnamon (1 tsp.)

Prep Technique:
1. Warm the oven to 350° Fahrenheit.
2. Combine each of the cookie fixings in a mixing container to form stiff dough.
3. Roll out the dough into 16 cookie balls (1.5-inch circles).
4. Combine the cinnamon and sweetener in a small dish. Roll the balls in the mixture until well coated.
5. Place on a parchment-lined cookie sheet and flatten slightly.
6. Bake for 15 minutes.
7. Remove and cool slightly before serving.

Strawberry Thumbprints

Servings Provided: 16

Cooking & Prep Time: 25-30 min.

Macro Counts For Each Serving:

- **Protein**: 2 g
- **Fat Content**: 9 g
- **Calories**: 95
- **Total Net Carbs**: 1 g

Ingredient List:

- Almond flour (1 cup)
- Baking powder (.5 tsp.)
- Coconut flour (2 tbsp.
- Salt (.5 tsp.)
- Cinnamon (.5 tsp.)
- Sugar-free strawberry jam (2 tbsp.)
- Shredded coconut (1 tbsp.)
- Erythritol (.5 cup)
- Whisked eggs (2)
- Coconut oil (4 tbsp.)
- Almond extract (.5 tsp.)
- Vanilla extract (.5 tsp.)

Prep Technique:

1. Set the oven temperature to 350º Fahrenheit.
2. Cover a cookie tin with a sheet of parchment paper.
3. Whisk the dry fixings and make a hole in the middle. Combine and fold in the wet fixings to form dough. Break it into 16 segments and roll into balls.
4. Arrange each one on the prepared cookie sheet and bake 15 minutes.
5. When done; cool completely, and add a dab of jam to each one with a sprinkle of coconut.

Walnut Cookies

Servings Provided: 16

Cooking & Prep Time: 20 min.

Macro Counts For Each Serving:

- **Protein**: 3 g
- **Fat Content**: 6.7 g
- **Calories**: 72
- **Total Net Carbs**: 1.1 g

Ingredient List:

- Ground cinnamon (1 tsp.)
- Erythritol (2 tbsp.)
- Egg (1)

- Ground walnuts (1.5 cups)

Prep Technique:

1. Set the oven temperature to reach 350° Fahrenheit.
2. Finely grind the nuts, leaving medium-sized pieces to your liking.
3. Combine the cinnamon and erythritol with the egg. Fold in the walnuts.
4. Shape into balls and place onto a parchment paper-lined baking tin.
5. Bake for 10 to 13 minutes.

Walnut & Orange Cookies

Servings Provided: 10

Cooking & Prep Time: 60 min.

Macro Counts For Each Serving:

- **Protein**: 7 g
- **Fat Content**: 17 g
- **Calories**: 137
- **Total Net Carbs**: 4 g

Ingredient List:

- Walnut halves (8 oz.)

- Orange - zested (3 tbsp.)
- Eggs (1)
- Stevia drops (20)
- Cinnamon to garnish (1 pinch)
- Shredded coconut - to garnish (to your liking)

Prep Technique:

1. Set the oven temperature to 320º Fahrenheit.
2. Toast the walnuts for about 10 minutes until browned. Add them to a food processor. Toss in the rest of the fixings and continue blending until it's smooth.
3. Shape into ten balls and slightly flatten. Drizzle with a portion of the shredded coconut.
4. Bake for 40 minutes. Cool on a few minutes and add to a platter to finish cooling.
5. Store in an airtight container to enjoy any time.

White Chocolate Macadamia Nut Cookies

Servings Provided: 38 cookies

Cooking & Prep Time: 25 min.

Macro Counts For Each Serving:

- **Protein**: 7.8 g
- **Fat Content**: 9 g

- **Calories**: 91
- **Total Net Carbs**: 0.8 g

Ingredient List:
- Vanilla extract (1 tsp.)
- Sukrin:1 or Swerve (.5 cup)
- Softened butter (.5 cup)
- Egg (1)
- Almond flour (1 cup)
- Coconut flour (.25 cup)
- Unflavored whey protein (2 tbsp.)
- Baking powder (1 tsp.)
- Salt (.5 tsp.)
- Chopped low-carb white chocolate bar (4 oz.)
- Coarsely chopped macadamia nuts (5 oz.)

Prep Technique:
1. Use an electric mixer to cream the butter and the sweetener. Toss in and mix the egg and vanilla.
2. In another mixing container, whisk the almond flour with the salt, coconut flour, whey powder, and baking powder.
3. Stir the dry mix into the wet mix. Fold in the white chocolate and macadamia nuts.

4. Scoop by tablespoonful's of batter onto a silicone or parchment paper-lined baking pans.
5. Bake at 325-350° Fahrenheit for 8 to 10 minutes (edges should be browned).
6. Cool for five minutes, and transfer each cookie to wire rack to cool completely.
7. Store covered in refrigerator. They are best served the next day (they'll be crumbly right after baking).

Chapter 8: A Final Word - Keto-Friendly Essentials

Grains to Avoid:

First, you need to realize grains are made from carbohydrates. This list is based on one cup servings. Avoid bread, pasta, pizza crusts, or crackers and cookies made with these grains:

- **Buckwheat:** 33 carbs - 6 protein - 1 grams fat
- **Wheat:** (1 slice wheat bread) 14 carbs - 3 protein - 1 gram fat
- **Barley:** 44 carbs - 4 protein - 1 gram fat
- **Quinoa:** 39 carbs - 8 protein - 4 grams fat
- **Corn:** 32 carbs - 4 protein - 1 grams fat
- **Millet:** 41 carbs - 6 protein - 2 grams fat
- **Bulgur:** 33 carbs - 5.6 protein - 0.4 grams fat
- **Amaranth:** 46 carbs - 9 protein - 4 grams fat
- **Oats:** 36 carbs - 6 protein - 3 grams fat
- **Rice:** 45 carbs - 5 protein - 2 grams fat
- **Rye:** 15 carbs - 3 protein - 1 gram fat

Added Sugar: The sugars to avoid include maltose,

dextrose, corn syrup, and maltodextrin. If you see these 'sugar' items, be aware:

- Beet
- Brown
- Cane
- Castor
- Coconut
- Coconut palm
- Confectioner's
- Corn
- Date
- Granulated
- Palm
- Powdered
- Raw
- Turbinado
- Yellow

High-Fructose Corn Syrup: These are some of the ones you need to avoid:

- Brown rice
- Buttered
- Corn syrup & solids

- Golden
- High fructose corn
- High maltose corn
- Malt
- Refiner's
- Rice

Honey: High-quality honey contains antioxidants and nutrients, making it a <u>better choice</u> than refined sugar. However, it's still high in calories and carbs and may not be suitable for a Keto diet.

Maple Syrup: Each serving of maple syrup packs a good amount of micronutrients like manganese and zinc but is also high in sugar and carbs. Maple Syrup is 14 grams

Maltodextrin: This highly processed sweetener is produced from starchy plants like rice, corn or wheat and contains the <u>same</u> amount of calories and carbs as regular sugar.

Unhealthy Processed Vegetable Oils:

You may wonder why using these oils are so bad since they all maintain zero carbs but they do have up to 14 grams of fat each per one tablespoon.

- Soybean
- Corn
- Canola
- Grapeseed
- Peanut
- Sunflower
- Sesame
- Safflower

Trans fats are bad for your cholesterol levels. They increase the levels of LDL (bad) cholesterol and decrease your levels of HDL (good) cholesterol, and also may raise your triglyceride levels. Eating too many omega-6 fatty acids can increase your risk of developing blood clots, and has also been linked to increased risk for various types of cancer. When oil oxidizes it reacts with oxygen, forming harmful free radicals and toxic compounds. That's why oils which oxidize easily shouldn't be used for cooking.

Foods Included Using The Ketogenic Plan

You will find the basic food items you will need to use on the Keto plan in this segment.

Excellent Keto-Friendly Flour Substitutes:

Almond flour: Prepare a batch of this healthy gluten-free baking by blanching the almonds in a pot of boiling water. Remove the skins. Grind the almonds into a fine flour to use for baking low-carb cookies, cakes, and pie crusts. Almond flour is a suitable replacement and is used as all-purpose flour. Each ¼ cup portion is only 6 carbs per gram, 150 calories, 3 net carbs, and 11 grams of fat which make it an excellent Keto-friendly option.

Coconut Flour: Use the coconut option for your Keto baking needs which contains only 3 grams of net carbs and 4 grams of protein for two tablespoons. You can add oils, eggs, and other liquids as needed. Like fiber, protein helps you stay full longer.

Flax Meal: Bake the delicious fiber into your recipes at 13 grams for just two tablespoons. Keep it refrigerated for freshness. You will receive about 4.25 cups per pound of the meal. Its nutty taste also provides benefits for your digestive tract with its natural nutrients.

Sunflower Seed Meal: You only gain 5 net carbs for each one-ounce serving. Use the same amount of sunflower seed meal as you do with almond meal flour since they have very similar properties. You also gain essential minerals and vitamins, including vitamin E, copper, selenium, phosphorus, and thiamine.

Psyllium Husks: Psyllium is a form of fiber and sometimes called ispaghula. It is known as a laxative as well as its benefits to your pancreas and heart. You will set it in some of your bread recipes.

Oat Fiber: is important because it gives a great bread-like texture. Oat Fiber is made from grinding the oat's outer husk which is pure insoluble fiber. Therefore, the fiber isn't broken down in the digestive tract or dissolved in water. Several recipes have this ingredient which is Keto-friendly with its low-carb components.
Note: Oat fiber isn't the same as oat flour which is made from grinding the oats.

Healthy Choices For Seeds & Nuts

Fresh Seeds: Pumpkin seeds are a great source of magnesium for you. They help immensely with your blood sugar levels and muscles. Flax seeds are another great source for omega-3 fatty acids. The micronutrients found in flax help reduce inflammation in your body. Coconut is also a good choice which can be used as shredded and unsweetened. These are a few more to consider with the approximate carbs listed:

- **Sesame Seeds -** 9 grams - 1 tbsp. (2.1 grams of carbs)
- **Flaxseeds -** 10.3 grams - 1 tbsp. (3 grams of carbs)
- **Chia Seeds -** 28.4 grams or 1 oz. (12 grams of carbs)
- **Coconut -** 1 medium - 397 grams (60 grams of carbs)

Fresh Nuts: Nuts have more minerals than many other foods. For Brazil nuts: The Brazil nuts are very high in selenium which is important for your immune system. It also assists your thyroid function. Add the Brazil nuts to snack time for your daily needs of selenium. Walnuts are an excellent source for protein, omega-3 fatty acids, and fiber. The combo will fill you up and prevent blood sugar spikes. These are a few with the approximate carbs listed:

- **Pecans -** per nut (.09 grams)
- **Hazelnuts -** 10 nuts - (.94 grams net carbs)
- **Almonds -** 1 ounce - (2.9 grams net carbs)
- **Walnuts -** 7 whole nuts (2 grams net carbs)
- **Pine Nuts -** 1 oz. or 28.35 grams (2.4 grams net carbs)
- **Cashews -** 18 kernels or 1 oz. (7.7 grams net carbs)
- **Pistachios -** .25 cup or 28 grams (5 grams net carbs)
- **Macadamia Nuts -** .25 cup (.23 grams net carbs)

Dairy-Free Substitutions:

Almond Milk

The delicious milk is made from grinding and mixing the

almonds with water and running them through a filtering mixture. The nutty flavor is also enriched with minerals, vitamins, and protein including riboflavin, calcium, as well as vitamin D and E.

One cup of sweetened coconut milk is about 6 grams compared to 1 cup of unsweetened, which has <u>3.38</u> grams of carbs. A cup of unsweetened coconut milk contains 11.86 grams of fat, so you're adding to the Keto cause.

Unsweetened Coconut Milk

Research has indicated coconut milk is beneficial for the effects on your immune system, heart health, and for weight loss. For <u>one cup</u> of raw, canned milk is 48 grams of fat, 6 carbs, and 445 calories. Keep in mind, the nutritional content may vary between brands. Canned coconut milk usually has a creamy - thick consistency. It is an excellent Keto option for people who typically use it for cooking and baking.

Flax Milk

This is a relatively new choice which is loaded with omega-3 fatty acids which aid with heart disease, strokes, diabetes, and cancer. It's also gluten-free as well as vitamins, D, B12, and A. For <u>one cup/</u>one ounce, unsweetened flax milk you will have 1 carb and just 30 calories with 2 grams of fat.

Butters:

Cashew butter

Used in moderation, it is a healthy addition to your baking goods. The butter is usually sold in its raw form, requiring refrigeration once the package is opened.

Use caution because it has <u>94 calories </u>for one tbsp. as well as 8 grams of fat. Using it in moderation of no more than one or two tablespoons daily to help you feel more satisfied and fuller to help prevent you from overeating. It can provide you with potassium beta carotene, lutein, vitamin K, selenium, copper, and zinc.

Ghee

Put in a stock of ghee as a great staple for your clarified butter.

Melted Coconut Oil

Coconut oil is also used as one of the best ways to improve ketone levels in people with nervous system disorders, such as those with Alzheimer's disease. The oil contains medium-chain triglycerides (MCTs) which speed up the ketosis process. Unlike many other fats, the MCTs are absorbed rapidly and go directly to the liver where they are used for immediate energy – resulting in conversion to ketones.

The oil contains four types of these fats, 50% of which comes from lauric acid. Research has indicated the higher percentage may produce sustained ketosis levels because it is metabolized more gradual than other MCTs. Add coconut oil slowly to your diet because it can cause some stomach cramping or diarrhea until you adjust. Begin with one teaspoon daily, and work it up to two to three tablespoons over the span of about one week.

Avocado Oil

Avocado oil is beneficial for your blood cholesterol levels. It is high in an antioxidant (lutein) which is also a carotenoid found naturally in your eyes. You will reduce the risk of common age-related diseases while lowering the risk of cataracts.

Macadamia Oil

One of the benefits of this oil is that it has a high smoke point. It carries a mild flavor which is a super alternative to olive oil in mayonnaise.

Add MCT Oils

Your Ketogenic experience can improve with the use of medium-chain triglycerides (MCT oil). These exclusive fatty acids are found in their natural form in palm and coconut oil. You will notice some of the smoothies use this as a component. These are just a few of the examples:

- The oil helps lower your blood sugar.
- The use of MCTs makes it much easier to get into – and remain - in ketosis.
- It is a natural anti-convulsive.
- It is also excellent for appetite control and weight loss.

Low-Carb Sweeteners Guide:

Monkfruit Sweetener:

Monk fruit, or *lo han guo*, is a small green melon native to southern China. It gets its name from the monks who first cultivated it many centuries ago. Monk fruit sweetener can be used anywhere you would use regular sugar. This fruit sweetener is a natural sweetener native to southern China and is extracted from the monk fruit plant. Monk fruit extract contains zero carbs and calories, making it a great option for a Ketogenic diet. The amount you use can vary between different brands based on what other ingredients may be included in the particular recipe used. It also holds anti-inflammatory properties, promotes weight loss, and is safe for those with diabetes.

Erythritol (powder)

Enjoy this as a natural low-calorie sweetener without the added calories. Erythritol belongs to a class of compounds called sugar alcohols which include maltitol, sorbitol, and xylitol. It contains 70% of the sweetness with 0.24 calories per gram compared to 4 calories in table sugar. However, because of its chemical structure, you may have digestive issues if consumed in large quantities. One of its deeming qualities is that it does not raise your blood sugar levels.

Swerve granular sweetener

This is a super Keto-friendly choice and is certified non-GMO, zero net carbs, zero calories, and non-glycemic. It will not raise your blood sugar and measures cup-for-cup just like sugar. It can be purchased in confectioners and granular forms. For convenience, it also is sold in individual packages. It is also an excellent baking option with a composition of natural flavors, oligosaccharides, and erythritol. It carries 0.2 calories per teaspoon with 60 to 80% of the sweetness of sugar.

Pyure Granulated Stevia
The blend of stevia and erythritol is an excellent alternative to baking, sweetening desserts, and various cooking needs. For a ½ tsp. (2 grams) serving, you will have 2 grams of carbs and zero calories. The substitution ratio is one teaspoon of sugar for each one-third tsp. of Pyure. Add slowly and adjust to your taste since you can always add a bit more. If you need powdered sugar, just grind the sweetener in a high-speed blender such as a NutriBullet until it's very dry.

Xylitol (granulated)
Xylitol is also known to keep mouth bacteria in check which goes a long way to protect your dental health. It has 40% fewer calories than sugar and is found naturally in veggies and fruits. Steer on the side of caution because it does have laxative properties. If you

have a dog, be sure to use caution since it is toxic to dogs.

Yacon Syrup (liquid)

Substitute yacon syrup using an equal amount in place of other liquid sweeteners like molasses, corn syrup or cane juice. Since your body doesn't digest a large portion of yacon syrup, it contains about one-third the calories of regular sugar, with just 20 calories per tablespoon (15 ml). Additionally, though it has about 11 grams of carbs per tablespoon (15 ml), both human and animal studies have found that yacon syrup may help reduce blood sugar and insulin levels to promote blood sugar control.

Other Essential Items:

Fresh Organic Eggs

Eggs create additional moisture and structure for a tasty batter for any delicious bread item you are creating. Many chefs boast the fresher the egg, the most flavorful results. Keep them fresh longer by storing them to the back of the fridge, not in the door. However, Taste of Home put it to the test and discovered the age of the eggs did not make a difference over the success of a baked cake.

Mozzarella Cheese

The delicious mozzarella is easily grated which makes it an excellent choice for your baking needs. It has four simple ingredients including salt, citric acid, rennet, and milk (cow or buffalo). You will enjoy it more know it only has 2.2 grams of carbs for 100 grams. 22 fats, and 22 grams of protein.

Garlic

Use garlic whenever possible to acquire its potent medicinal properties. It is related to leeks, shallots, and onions with each segment of the bulb called the clove. Each bulb can provide ten to twenty cloves. It is very nutritious with 9 grams of carbs, 42 calories, and 1.8 grams of protein. It contains manganese, B6, and vitamin C, as well as varied other nutrients.

Mozzarella Cheese

The delicious mozzarella is easily grated which makes it an excellent choice for your baking needs. It has four simple ingredients including salt, citric acid, rennet, and milk (cow or buffalo). You will enjoy it more know it only has 2.2 grams of carbs for 100 grams. 22 fats, and 22 grams of protein.

Pumpkin:

Include pumpkin in your 'must-have' list. It's full of essential minerals and vitamins including B1, B6, and PP. Carotenes are also in abundance with vitamin A. It has been noted that pumpkin is about 4.5 times higher in vitamin A than carrots. You will notice some of the bread recipes will incorporate pumpkin into its list.

Conclusion

I hope you have enjoyed the many ways to prepare Keto bread using healthier methods. You have the tools to go from scratch to a masterpiece.

This book has been written by standards in the United States. You are fortunate that so many recipes are now available online. If you use the metric system, you can be faced with other challenges. You can use this site: (http://www.rapidtables.com/convert/temperature/how -celsius-to-fahrenheit.htm) to switch Celsius into Fahrenheit if you need to convert the recipe.

You have the basics of what the plan is, but now it's time to understand some of the pitfalls of the method. However, each of the issues is an indication that your body is in ketosis. These are a few of the signs you will observe as you begin the transition:

- You may experience what is called the 'induction flu' or 'Keto flu' which involves lowered mental functions and energy.
- You may suffer from sleeping issues, bouts of

nausea, increased hunger, or other possible digestive worries.

- Several days into the plan should remedy these effects.
- If not, add 1/2 of a teaspoon of salt to a glass of water and drink it to help with the side effects.
- You may need to do this once a day in the first week, and it could take about 15 to 20 minutes before it helps.
- It will improve with time.

You may also notice an aroma similar to nail polish. Not surprising, because this is acetone, a ketone product. It may also give you a unique body odor as your body adjusts to the diet changes. Maintain good oral health and use a breath refresher if needed.

Leg cramps may be an issue as you begin ketosis. The loss of magnesium (a mineral) can be a demon and create a bit of pain with the onset of the Keto diet plan changes. With the loss of the minerals during urination, you could experience bouts of cramps in your legs.

Remember, these are just possibilities.

This is what *Katie Courie,* the former *Today Show* host shared to Instagram:

"So I've been doing the Keto diet for a week now and I actually do feel better. The fourth or fifth day, I felt a little shaky and headachy, but I feel much better." She experienced the 'Keto flu' which is a typical side effect of the plan. It is always best to have a physician's advice before beginning the Keto way of eating.

Let's have a treat before you get started on your delicious bread-related items.

Smoothie In A Bowl

Servings Provided: 1

Cooking & Prep Time: 4-5 min.

Macro Counts For Each Serving:

- **Protein**: 35
- **Fat Content**: 35g
- **Calories**: 570
- **Total Net Carbs**: 4 g

Ingredient List:

- Almond milk (.5 cup)
- Spinach (1 cup)

- Heavy cream (2 tbsp.)
- Low-carb protein powder (1 scoop)
- Coconut oil (1 tbsp.)
- Ice (2 cubes)

Ingredient List - The Toppings:
- Walnuts (4)
- Raspberries (4)
- Chia seeds (1 tsp.)
- Shredded coconut (1 tbsp.)

Prep Technique:
1. Add a cup of spinach to your high-speed blender. Pour in the cream, almond milk, ice, and coconut oil.
2. Blend for a few seconds until it has an even consistency, and all ingredients are well combined. Empty the goodies into a serving dish.
3. Arrange your toppings or give them a toss and mix them together. Of course, make it pretty and alternate the strips of toppings.

How did that taste?

Finally, if you found this book useful in any way, a review on Amazon is always appreciated!

Index For The Recipes

Chapter 2: Keto Bread Favorites

1. Almond-Coconut Flour Bread

2. Coconut Flaxseed Bread

3. Cottage Bread

4. Dinner Rolls

5. Garlic Focaccia

6. Macadamia Bread

7. Pork Rind Bread

8. Sesame Seed Bread

Sweet Bread

1. Apple Cider Donut Bites

2. Banana Bread

3. Blueberry - Lemon Bread

4. Chocolate Croissants

5. Cranberry Bread - Gluten-Free

6. Cream Cheese Coffee Cake

7. Delicious Plain Cheese Croissants

8. Raspberry Cream Cheese Coffee Cake – Slow Cooked

9. Walnut Bread

Chapter 3: Keto Bagels

1. Almond Flour Gluten-Free Bagels
2. Blueberry Cream Cheese Bagels
3. Blueberry Yeast Bagels
4. Cinnamon Raisin Bagels
5. Cinnamon Sugar Bagels
6. Coconut Fathead Bagels
7. Coconut - Garlic Bagels
8. Croissant Bagels
9. Delicious Almond Fathead Bagels
10. French Toast Bagel
11. Mozzarella Dough Bagels
12. Onion Bagels
13. Rosemary Bagels

Chapter 4: Keto Pizzas

1. Almond Flour Pizza Crust
2. BBQ Chicken Pizza
3. BBQ Meat-Lovers Pizza
4. Bell Pepper Pizza
5. Breakfast Pizza Waffles

6. Buffalo Chicken Crust Pizza

7. Margherita Keto Pizza

8. Pepperoni Pizza

9. Pizza Bites

10.   Pocket Pizza

11.   Sausage Crust Pizza

12.   Thai Chicken Flatbread Pizza

13.   Zucchini Pizza Bites

Flatbread & Pita Bread Options

1. Cheese Flatbread

2. Matzo Bread - Jewish Flatbread

3. Pita Pizza

Chapter 5: Keto Crackers & Breadsticks

1. Cheddar Parmesan Chips

2. Tortilla Chips

Crackers

1. Almond Crackers

2. Buttery Pesto Crackers

3. Chia Seed Crackers

4. Graham Crackers

5. Healthy Goat Cheese Crackers

6. Hemp Heart Crackers

7. Salty Butter Crackers

8. Rosemary & Sea Salt Flax Crackers

9. Super-Easy TJ Keto Crackers

10. Toasted Sesame Crackers

Breadsticks

1. Cheesy Garlic Breadstick Bites

2. Coconut & Flax Breadsticks

3. Italian Breadsticks

4. Oat Sticks

5. 3-Way Tasty Breadsticks - Cheesy - Italian - Cinnamon Sugar

Chapter 6: Keto Muffin Specialties

Sweet Options

1. Apple Almond Muffins

2. Applesauce - Cinnamon & Nutmeg Muffins

3. Banana & Applesauce Muffins

4. Blackberry Lemon Muffins

5. Blueberry Cream Cheese Muffins

6. Brownie Muffins

7. Chocolate Chip Covered Muffins

8. Chocolate Hazelnut Muffins

9. Chocolate Zucchini Muffins

10. Coconut Flour Cranberry Pumpkin Muffins

11. Coconut Lemon Muffins

12. Coffee Cake Muffins

13. Double Chocolate Blender Muffins

14. English Muffin

15. French Toast Muffins

16. Gingerbread Blender Muffins

17. Lemon Poppyseed Muffins

18. Pancake & Berry Muffins

19. Pumpkin Cream Cheese Muffins

20. Pumpkin Maple Flaxseed Muffins

21. Pumpkin Spice Mug Muffin

22. Strawberry Glazed Muffins

Other Options

1. Cauliflower Bacon & Cheese Muffins

2. Coconut Bacon Egg Muffins

3. Cornbread Muffins

4. Green Eggs & Ham Muffins

5. Jalapeno Muffins

6. Lemon Poppyseed Muffins

7. Onion & Squash Muffins

Chapter 7: Keto Cookies

1. Almond Nut Butter Cookies

2. Almond Shortbread Cookies

3. Chocolate Macaroon Cookies With Coconut

4. Chocolate & Orange Cookies

5. Chocolate Sea Salt Cookies

6. Chocolate Zucchini Cookies

7. Cinnamon Cookies

8. Coconut No-Bake Cookies

9. Coconut & Chocolate Cookies

10.   Dark Chocolate Chip Cookies

11.   Italian Almond Macaroons

12.   Italian Amaretti Cookies

13.   Low-Carb Chocolate Chip Cookies

14.   Orange Cream Cheese Cookies & Nuts

15.   Peanut Butter Cookies

16.   Peanut Butter & Jelly Cookies

17.   Pistachio Cookies

18.   Pumpkin Cheesecake Cookies

19.   Snickerdoodles

20.   Strawberry Thumbprints

21.   Walnut Cookies

22.   Walnut & Orange Cookies

23.   White Chocolate Macadamia Nut Cookies

Made in the USA
Monee, IL
07 May 2020